Forts & Palaces
of India

Forts
&
Palaces
of
India

Sentinels of History

BINDU MANCHANDA

Lustre Press
Roli Books

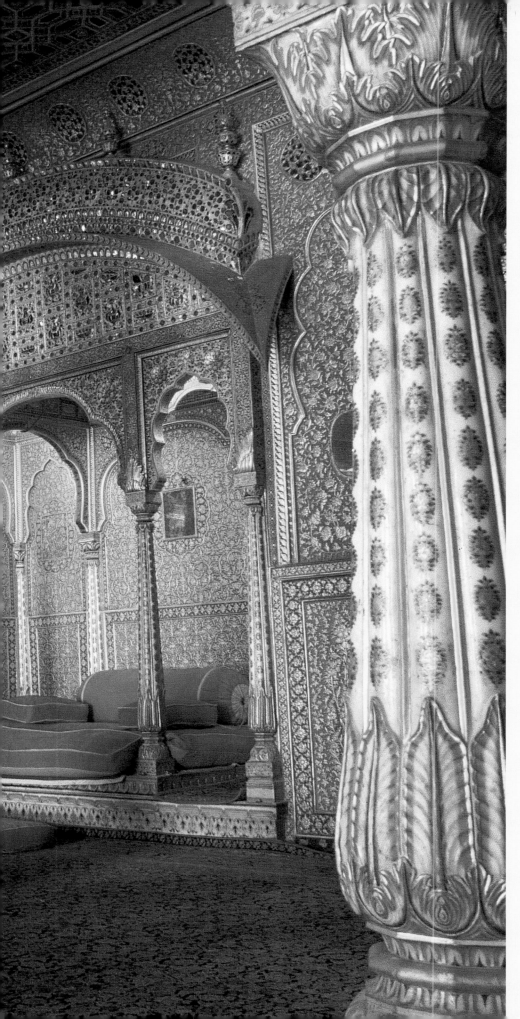

CONTENTS

ACKNOWLEDGEMENTS

I would like to thank INTACH, especially the Chairman, Mr S. K. Misra, Member Secretary Mr Dalip Mehta, Dr O. P. Agrawal, and my colleagues Mr Janhwij Sharma and Mr Divay Gupta for their support. I am also grateful to INTACH for allowing me access to their library and documents.

A special thank you to Raja Chandra Vijay Singh and Rani Sushma Kumari of Sahspur-Bilari for their guidance.

I would also like to acknowledge and thank for their help: Maharaja Gaj Singh and Princess Shivranjini Raje of Jodhpur, Maharani Priyadarshini Raje Scindia of Gwalior, Maharawal Brijraj Singh of Jaisalmer, Maharaj Sangram Sinh Gaekwad of Baroda and Thakur Sunder Singh of Sodawas.

My sincere appreciation and gratitude for their help to: Dharmendra Kanwar for Jaipur, Shobita Punja for Orccha, Nalini Thakur for Kangla, R.R. Mahinder Singh for Nagaur, Harshad Kumari of Jamnagar and the Mehrangarh Museum Trust.

I am especially grateful to Martand Singh for sharing his immense knowledge on the subject, and to my colleagues Anil Browne and Meenu Sharma without whose help this book would not have been possible. A big thank you to Dipa Chaudhuri, Himanshu Bhagat and Priya Kapoor of Roli Books for advice and support.

PRECEDING PAGES 2-3: *A ROOM IN THE LAKE PALACE, UDAIPUR, RAJASTHAN.*
PAGES 4-5: *KARAN MAHAL, JUNAGARH FORT, BIKANER, RAJASTHAN.*
FACING PAGE: *DETAIL FROM SAMODE PALACE, SAMODE, RAJASTHAN.*
FOLLOWING PAGES 10-11: *AMBER FORT, JAIPUR, RAJASTHAN.*
PAGES 12-13: *SUNLIGHT ILLUMINATES THE MONSOON PALACE NEAR UDAIPUR, RAJASTHAN.*

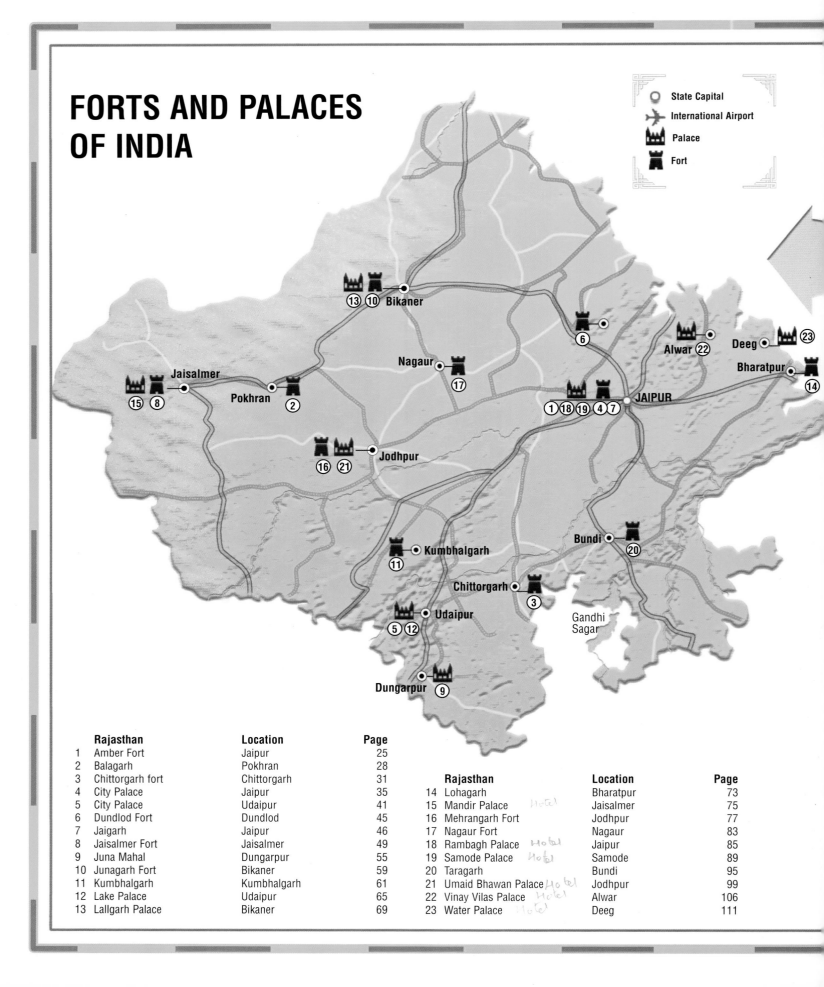

FORTS AND PALACES OF INDIA

State Capital
International Airport
Palace
Fort

13 10 **Bikaner**

6

22 **Alwar** 22 **Deeg** 23

Bharatpur 14

Nagaur 17

Jaisalmer 15 8

Pokhran 2

JAIPUR 1 18 19 4 7

16 21 **Jodhpur**

Bundi 20

11 **Kumbhalgarh**

Chittorgarh 3

Udaipur 5 12

Gandhi Sagar

Dungarpur 9

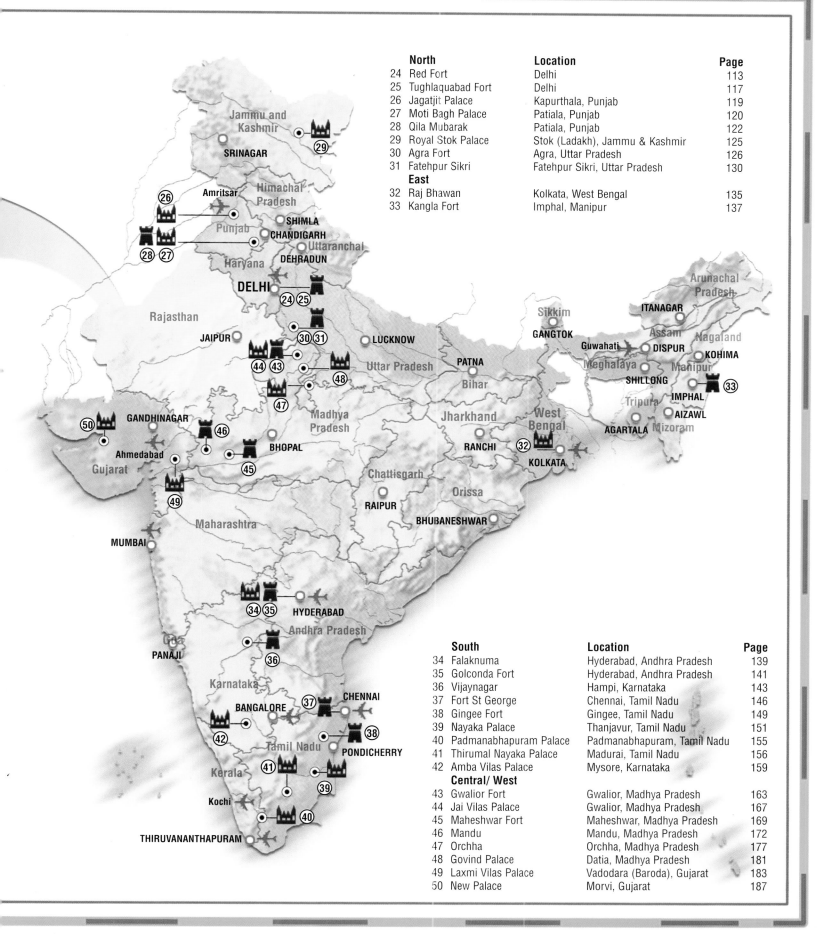

INDIA

THE LAND OF FORTS AND PALACES

India has one of the world's oldest civilizations, which can be traced back to at least 5,000 years. Fittingly, India is a treasure trove of monuments of historical and archaeological significance. One legacy of this rich and varied history—going far back into early antiquity—is the numerous forts and palaces, which dot the landscape through the length and breadth of India. In popular imagination forts and palaces are redolent of mystique, romance, pleasure and intrigue; but above all—melding beauty and grace with strength and substance—these proud sentinels are living reminders of India's breathtakingly rich civilization and culture.

ANCIENT LEGACY

The earliest reference to forts and palaces in India can be found in the Vedas—the collection of Sanskrit hymns composed approximately around 1100 BC. The Vedic hymns mention *pur* several times, which could refer to a rampart or a fort or a stronghold. The Vedic deity Indra is specially referred to as Purandara or 'destroyer of forts'. Historians aver that the *pur* that the Vedas refer to were in fact the defensive structures built by the inhabitants of the Harappa or the Indus Valley Civilization, and Indra's 'rending forts as age consumes a garment' is a reference to the invading Aryan hordes who, in all likelihood, overran the remnants of the Harappan civilization.

FACING PAGE: THE 15TH CENTURY KUMBHALGARH FORT, RAJASTHAN, BUILT BY RANA KUMBHA.

Other notable references to forts in ancient texts include those in the *Arthashastra*, the 4th-century classic on statecraft attributed to Kautilya; the *Vastushastra*, the ancient manuals on town planning and architecture; and in the *Mayamata*, the south-Indian treatise on architecture written sometime between the 9th and the 12th century.

The earliest surviving forts in India date back to the 8th century AD. A notable example is the fort at Chittorgarh in Rajasthan, which was built in AD 728. Most of India's surviving forts, however, were built from the 12th century onwards, like the Jaisalmer Fort in Rajasthan and the Golconda Fort near Hyderabad. While hardly any forts and palaces built before the 12th century remain standing, there is ample evidence that they existed from accounts left by travellers, archeological finds, ancient cave paintings, as well as mention in ancient texts and treatises on architecture and statecraft.

The great Indian epics Mahabharata and Ramayana, composed between 900 - 520 BC, have many references to forts and palaces. The Pandavas and Kauravas, clans of rival cousins in the Mahabharata are described as, 'living in pillared pavilions and marble halls, with opulent interiors and highly polished floors.' The Pandavas established a kingdom in Indraprastha, said to be a part of the fortified Purana Quila complex in New Delhi. Archaeological evidence that a fairly sophisticated civilization flourished at the time is available in the form of remains of pottery and artefacts in sites throughout this region.

Megasthanes, the Greek ambassador to the court of Chandragupta Maurya in the 4th century BC describes the king's palace at Pataliputra as set amidst gardens, with a series of open halls supported by wooden columns decorated in gold and silver. The palace, according to him, surpassed the grandeur of the Achaemenid palaces of Susa and Ecbatana in Persia. The veracity of Megasthanes's account has been bolstered by recent excavations that have revealed some remains of the Mauryan palace in Patna, the present day city at the site of Pataliputra.

The cave temples of western Deccan, excavated and sculpted between 100 BC and 170 AD; the frescoes of Ajanta; the description of Emperor Harshavardhan's 'Raj Bhavan' or royal palace in the 7th century by Banbhatta in *Kadambari* and *Harshacharita*—all bear testimony to the fact that ancient India had many palaces and forts that were the envy of foreign travellers.

But why have none of them survived? Are the ravages of time the only explanation?

The reason could also lie in the Hindu belief that temples, as the abode of gods, were sacrosanct and had to be preserved at all costs, while palaces and homes, however beautiful, had a temporal and utilitarian role, and were therefore expendable. Another reason that there are no remains of palaces and forts from the ancient times could be the predominant use of wood as the basic material of construction, which made them susceptible to decay and destruction. Moreover, very often, rulers felt the need to build their own palaces, their own forts and even their own new capital, rather than maintain and restore those of their predecessors.

Indian rulers, whether Hindu, Muslim or Buddhist, closely followed the rules and conventions laid out in their respective texts, both religious and secular, in all aspects of their life. There has always existed in India a strong link between cosmology, astrology and architecture. Therefore places of worship, forts, palaces and even entire cities were planned, built and developed based on certain rules and principles.

According to *Vastushastras*, the royal city should be planned according to mandalas—sacred diagrams, which represent the cosmos in a miniature form.

Different zones within the mandala represent different levels of the universe, the most powerful being the central square. Not many palaces based strictly on the mandala system exist today, mostly because of later additions and extensions to them. Govind Mahal at Datia, an early-17th century residence of Bir Singh Deo is designed according to the twenty-five squares mandala. The central square consists of the king's audience hall and sleeping chambers. The city of Jaipur, built by Sawai Jai Singh in early-18th century was planned on the nine-mandala pattern, with the royal palace at the centre.

The *Arthashastra*, in addition to being the standard reference for statecraft, was also consulted when the royal residences were built; it gives precise information on the layout of the royal palaces and forts. The palace was to be divided into nine squares, with pathways running from east to west and north to south. The king's chambers occupy the central square, next to the temple. The *Mayamata* also gives precise descriptions of the arrangements of buildings within the palace complex. The inner sanctum consists of the altar for the god Brahma, with the king's and the queen's chambers on either side.

In addition to the instructions laid out in the texts, the style of fortification in ancient India was also

BIRTHDAY CELEBRATIONS OF MAHARAJAH GAJ SINGH II IN THE DINING HALL OF THE UMAID BHAWAN PALACE, JODHPUR.

influenced by the local climate and the terrain. Based on their systems of defense, the forts were divided into six categories:

(i) *Giri durg* or hill forts, such as Chittorgarh, which were considered the most impregnable.

(ii) *Vana durg,* which were protected by forests, like the Ranthambore Fort.

(iii) *Jala durg,* protected by water, such as the Sidi Fort in Janjeera and the Ghagron Fort in Rajasthan.

(iv) *Dhanna durg,* protected by the desert, such as the Jaisalmer Fort.

(v) *Mahi durg,* protected by thick mud walls, such as the Lohagarh in Bharatpur.

(vi) *Nara durg,* city forts that were protected by forces of loyal men, such as Qila Mubarak in Patiala and the Nagaur Fort in Rajasthan.

MEDIEVAL SPLENDOUR

A vastly clearer picture of forts and palaces emerges as we approach the medieval period of Indian history. Whereas there is hardly any archaeological evidence on Pataliputra and Kanauj, respectively the capitals of the Mauryan and the Gupta empires, there is no dearth of monuments in the capital cities of later empires, such as Delhi and Agra.

This has led many historians to declare that prior to the advent of the Muslims, which roughly coincides with the early centuries of the last millennia, India did not have a strong tradition of palace architecture. (Mahmud Ghazni first invaded India in 1001 AD; his numerous raids were followed, after a two-century lull, by the Mohammad Ghori's invasions, starting in 1192.) However G.H.R. Tillotson has effectively dispelled this belief in his seminal work, *The Rajput Palaces*, which clearly distinguishes between the Rajput style of palace architecture and the Mughal style. The palaces of Orchha and Datia for instance, built in the 16th century, are designed in the Rajput style, as distinct from the Mughal style.

The Rajput style of palace architecture was rooted deeply in the ancient Hindu tradition of secular architecture, though it did incorporate elements of temple design. It differs most significantly from the later Islamic architecture in the arrangement of parts, and the massing, planning and the location of the major palaces.

The typical Mughal palace consists of a number of formally placed separate buildings surrounded by a fort wall. The Rajput palace is usually built on a slope or on top of a hill, with the buildings massed together and contiguous. More often than not, they are situated within a fortress. This skill of massing buildings to produce an imposing visual effect is something that is absent in Islamic architecture.

In detailing too, there are differences underlying the similarities: the Islamic decorative forms are more elegant and use fine materials such as precious and semi-precious stones, whereas the Rajput decorations such as mural paintings, mirror-work and religious iconography in the palace interiors are based on local folk-art traditions.

Both the Hindu style and the Islamic style of architecture exerted an equal amount of influence on each other. This is not surprising considering that Hindu craftsmen were extensively if not exclusively employed to build many monuments by Muslim rulers. The chajja (angled eave) and the bracket, incorporated extensively in Mughal architecture, is a distinctly Hindu detail, whereas fluted columns and certain other forms of applied decoration used in Rajput architecture have purely Islamic origins. The bangaldar roof or bangle roof, adapted from the Bengali vernacular bamboo hut, is used in both Rajput and Muslim architecture, though it is a distinctly Hindu form. This intermingling of styles and techniques was mostly to be found in the details.

There are however very evident differences between the two styles that far outweigh the similarities.

According to Tillotson, possibly the single most important element introduced into late-Hindu secular architecture by the Indo-Islamic architectural tradition is the appearance of the true arch. It is only after the Muslim conquests that the traditional Hindu trabeate system, which consisted of horizontal beams or lintels, was slowly replaced by the true arch. The cusped arch however was used in Hindu architecture and appears in ancient temples such as the 8th century temple of Martand near Anantnag and the 10th century temple of Pandrethan, both in Kashmir. It is also found in the temple architecture in Khajuraho. However, it began to be used extensively only from the 18th century onwards, after its use was perfected by the Mughals, especially during the reign of Shah Jahan (r. 1627-58).

The medieval palaces were usually fortified, contained, protected and heavily secured, probably due to the relentless strife and invasions from the early-12th century onwards. It is only much later, in the 19th century, after signing of peace treaties between the native states of India and the British, that another distinct palace architectural style, popularly known as the Indo-Saracenic style, emerged.

THE MODERN ERA

The Indo-Saracenic style represents a fusion of Indo-Islamic and European architectural ideas. The treaties signed with the British ensured peace and left the Indian maharajas with caches of money that had earlier been spent on maintaining huge armies and waging wars. New palaces, modelled on the European style, started replacing the older ones and reflected the newly acquired tastes of the maharajas. The durbar halls were replaced by magnificent ballrooms, mural paintings were discarded for glittering chandeliers and heavily embroidered fabrics on low-style seating was replaced by French furniture.

THE IMPOSING FAÇADE OF THE UMAID BHAWAN PALACE, JODHPUR.

The British architect Samuel Swinton Jacob is credited with this revival. Palaces designed by him make abundant use of traditional features such as jalis (ornamented pierced stone-screen), jharokas (decorative projecting balcony), chattris (roof-top pavilion with dome or vault; funerary monument), cusped arches and bangle roofs. This 'neo-Rajput' style took a firm hold on the Indian maharaja's imagination and nearly all palaces built in this period were executed in this style. The result, despite being slightly idiosyncratic, was not without charm. The happy intermingling of western-style arcades and towers with jharokas and jalis resulted in some impressive palaces, like the Baroda Palace, which was designed by Charles Mant. In the 20th century came a new sensibility, the thoroughly modern art-deco style that can be seen in the palaces at Indore, and at Morvi in Gujarat that was designed by Eckart Muthesius.

Independence brought with it an end to palace building but not without a final triumph. Work on the Umaid Bhawan palace in Jodhpur, built on the design by Lanchester and Lodge of London, started in 1929 and the palace was ready only by 1944, equaling if not exceeding in magnificence the Viceroy's palace in New Delhi.

After the merger of the princely states with the Union of India in 1947 and with the abolition of the Privy Purse—annual remittances guaranteed by law, by the government of India to the princes whose states where absorbed into the Indian union—in 1970, the

THE GROUND FLOOR BAR AT THE ART-DECO NEW PALACE IN MORVI, GUJARAT.
FOLLOWING PAGES 22-23: *THE HIGHLY ORNATE SOBHA NIWAS IN THE CITY PALACE,*
JAIPUR SERVES AS THE MAHARAJA'S SITTING ROOM.

upkeep of the palaces became prohibitively expensive and suffered as a result. In the ensuing period many were abandoned or taken over by the government, while some continued to remain in private hands and serve as private residences of the erstwhile royals.

A lot of them have been converted into heritage hotels (with some sections being used as private residences). One of the best examples of a royal residence cum luxury hotel is the Umaid Bhawan palace in Jodhpur. A large part of the Jai Niwas in Gwalior continues to be occupied by the royal family of Scindias, while the Gaekwads retain Lakshmi Vilas in Baroda and the Wodeyars of Mysore still own a large section of the Mysore city palace.

Many palaces have been converted into museums under private or government management. Old palaces are also being used as administrative offices in many cities and towns. In the 19th century, many forts had ugly barracks erected within their compounds by the British to house soldiers and many of them are still occupied by the Indian army. The Red Fort in Delhi and the Kangla Fort in Assam have only recently been freed of the army's presence, and are now being restored.

The future of Indian forts and palaces seems to be brighter than what it was ten years ago. Both the government and the private owners are keenly aware of the need to maintain these priceless legacies from India's past, and also of their potential as revenue generating properties.

Organizations like INTACH (The Indian National Trust of Art and Cultural Heritage), the A.S.I. (Archeological Survey of India), and other heritage societies, private trusts and individuals are actively involved in conservation efforts. The forts and palaces of India are timeless and it is incumbent upon the present generation to preserve them for posterity.

AMBER FORT

Amber

BUILT 11th century and later
LOCATION Jaipur, Rajasthan
STYLE Rajput with Mughal
influences
DYNASTY Kacchwaha

The fortified complex of Amber is built on a hilltop overlooking the Maota Lake. It was the capital of the Kacchwaha Rajputs from the 12th century until they moved to Jaipur in 1727. The old 11th-century fort that stood here originally, was extensively added to by Man Singh (r 1592-1615), and the many beautiful buildings that were added by Jai Singh later (r 1621-67) are truly spectacular.

The Mughal influence is strong, both in the architecture as well as in the decorative elements. The main entrance to the historic fort is through Suraj Pol or the Sun Gate, which faces the rising sun, the sun being the Kacchwaha emblem. The gate's lofty arch, flanked by jharokas, leads to Jaleb Chowk, a huge courtyard which contained the guard's quarters and administrative offices. These have now been converted into souvenir shops and snack bars.

A flight of steps leads to the old Shitla Devi temple, the abode of the clan deity of the Kacchawahas. This small temple has solid silver doors and silver lamps. The idol of the deity was installed by Man Singh in 1604 and is placed in a small niche in front of a marble courtyard surrounded by delicate columns with cusped arches. Singh Pol or the Lion Gate leads to a small second court, situated at a higher level. One corner of the courtyard is occupied by the Diwan-i-Aam which was built by Jai Singh. It is surrounded by double columns on the outer periphery and extended brackets carved like elephants. Near it is the Sattais Katcheri, a colonnade of twenty-seven columns (hence the name *sattais* or twenty-seven) where the revenue records were maintained.

The Ganesh Pol, the gate painted with beautiful floral patterns, and the elephant-headed god Ganesh painted over its arch, dates from 1639. Sukh Mandir is a three-storey gateway that links to private apartments of the palace, and the Sohag Mandir, at the upper levels of the gateway, has pierced jallis (filigreed screens) for the ladies to observe the activities below.

After passing through Ganesh Pol, one comes to the third courtyard in the complex, which was added by Jai

FACING PAGE: THE AMBER FORT, NESTLED IN THE ARAVALI HILLS, JUST OUTSIDE THE CITY OF JAIPUR. IN THE BACK-GROUND, CROWNING THE HILL IS THE NAHARGARH FORT.

RIGHT: INTRICATE TRADITIONAL ARTWORK IN THE CORRIDORS - A HALLMARK OF INDIAN PALACES.

Singh. A formal garden with pavilions on both sides is laid here. There is Sukh Niwas on the west and, facing it on the opposite side, is the two-storey pavilion Jai Mandir, also known as the Diwan-i-Khas. The Sheesh Mahal is a glittering hall with intricate mirror-work patterns on the walls and ceilings, and is enclosed by verandahs on three sides. Coloured glass is set into niches and windows and, exemplifying the finest standards of Mughal-style craftsmanship, the lower walls have patterned panels in marble-relief, the oft repeated motif being bunched flowers in vases.

The Jas Mandir at the upper level was the king's private chamber. It has two octagonal domes and a curved vault in the centre; the interiors are decorated with ornate mirror work and painted panels. A small marble hammam or bathing chamber, and the dining hall form a part of the apartments linked to the chambers.

A maze of steps, ramps and passages lead to the zenana, which was originally Man Singh's palace. A rectangular chowk (courtyard), which once had a garden with a Mughal-style pavilion, is surrounded by apartments all around it. The Zenana Mahal has a plain exterior with a few jharokas that look down on an artificial lake towards the east. Two formal gardens are laid at this end of the fort: the Kesar Kyari Bagh, which has star-shaped flower beds and was actually intended for *kesar* (saffron) cultivation; and the Dilaram Bagh, built in 1568. Said to be a resting place for Akbar on his way to pilgrimage to Ajmer, the garden's name is a clever pun on the name of its architect Dilaram, which means heartsease.

BALAGARH

Pokhran

BUILT 14th century
LOCATION Pokhran, Rajasthan
STYLE Rajput & Mughal
DYNASTY Champawat

*FOLLOWING A PATTERN THAT WAS REPEATED WITH MANY
FORTS, BALAGRAH WAS ORIGINALLY A MUD FORT THAT
WAS LATER REPLACED BY A RED SANDSTONE STRUCTURE.*

Surrounded by sand, rocks and salt ranges, Pokhran or the 'place of fine mirages' is situated midway between Jodhpur and Jaisalmer on the ancient trade route that carried salt, silk and spices to Persia.

The citadel of Balagarh, first built in the 14th century, is situated in Pokhran, and members of the Champawat clan have been living here since the fort was built. The Champawats were the premier nobles of the Jodhpur court and were bestowed the title of 'Pradhan' in recognition of their loyalty and stature. Originally a mud fort that was replaced by a red sandstone structure, Balagarh's architecture is a typical blend of Rajput and Mughal styles that was favoured by the ruling elite at the time.

Its austere façade is lightened by a large intricately carved jharokha on top of the arched gateway with huge wood and iron doors. The courtyard inside has a small charbagh (formal walled garden) with private apartments on three sides. A large bright painting of the clan deity adorns one wall and delicately carved red sandstone jharokhas look out into the gardens.

Mangal Mahal, the reception hall on the ground floor lies to the right, its most distinctive feature being four octagonal jharokhas which look out into the hall. Mangal Mahal was where the Mughal emperor Humayun's visit to Pokhran was celebrated by the Thakurs of Pokhran. The fort has been restored and is now run as a heritage hotel.

CHITTORGARH
Chittorgarh

BUILT 12th-16th century
LOCATION Chittorgarh, Rajasthan
STYLE Rajput
DYNASTY Sisodia

Many legends and tales of the fabled Rajput valour originate from Chittorgarh, the original seat of the Sisodia dynasty. The Sisodias were known as Guhilots earlier, and their ancestor Bappa Rawal is said to have established himself at Chittorgarh during the 8th century. This formidable battle-scarred fort was the capital of the Sisodias until 1568, when they shifted to Udaipur.

The giant 700-acre fort sprawls across a 500-foot high, half-a-mile wide and three-mile long hill, rising abruptly from the surrounding plain. Its ruined palaces, temples and towers were witness to three sackings, and three instances of jauhar or mass immolation by women and children.

In 1303, Sultan Ala-ud-din Khilji of Delhi—who, legend has it, was besotted by the beauty of Queen Padmini, wife of Rawal Ratan Singh I— laid siege to the fort. A fierce battle ensued in which more than 50,000 warriors died and Padmini, along with the women and children in the fort, committed jauhar.

The fort was also attacked by Bahadur Shah of Gujarat in 1535, and by the Mughal emperor Akbar in 1567. The Rajputs claimed it back after the first two sackings, but the third, by Akbar, was final. When the victorious Mughals entered the fort, they were confronted by the sight of hundreds of sacrificial pyres on which the families of the Sisodia warriors had

THE RUINS OF THE FAMED FORT OF CHITTOR. A SYMBOL OF RAJPUT VALOUR, CHITTORGARH WAS THE CAPITAL OF SISODIAS FROM WHERE THEY RULED OVER MEWAR FOR SIX CENTURIES BEFORE SHIFTING TO UDAIPUR.

immolated themselves. The entire deserted complex was engulfed in smoke.

Chittorgarh fort is entered through seven enormous spiked gates. The oldest surviving palace is that of Rana Kumbha's (r. 1433-68), who is credited with building the fort's stone ramparts and many temples within it, as well as the nine-storeyed Vijay Stambha or the Victory Tower to celebrate his victory over the sultan of Malwa in 1437.

Rana Kumbha's palace is approached through two gateways: first the immense Badi Pol and then the Tripolia, which is not three bays wide as the name suggests, but three bays deep. The gate leads to a large open court and on to the Darikhana or Sabha, a raised, columned hall. The Sabha conceals the main entrance to the private apartments. The largest surviving portion is the palace for the heir apparent, the Kunwar Pada. The zenana, identified by the jallis, is attached to the west side.

Great antiquity is claimed for some of the ruins and temples within the fort, though the palaces of Bhim and Padmini, in fact, date to the late-19th century and were most probably recreated at the original site. Situated in the middle of a lotus pond, Queen Padmini's palace is an early example of a pleasure palace, and contains within it the mirror in which Ala-ud-din Khilji supposedly saw Padmini's reflection. Historians however aver that the Rajputs would never have agreed to such a condition.

The palace of Rana Ratan Singh (r. 1528-31) is another important structure situated next to a small lake. The palace is built on a regular plan, but its interiors are irregular, consisting of a maze of small apartments, much like Rana Kumbha's palace. Nearby, in the 19th-century Fateh Prakash Palace, an in-house museum has displays of weapons, sculptures, artifacts and some folk art. Among the last palaces to be built in Chittor before the Sisodias shifted to Udaipur, were those of the two war heroes of the siege of 1567, Patta and Jaimal.

THE VIJAYA STAMBH OR VICTORY TOWER STANDS IN
SILENT VIGIL OVER THE RUINS OF CHITTORGARH.
FACING PAGE: PADMINI'S PALACE, CHITTOR.

CITY PALACE

Jaipur

BUILT 1727
LOCATION Jaipur, Rajasthan
BUILT BY Sawai Jai Singh II
STYLE Rajput
DYNASTY Kacchwaha

On 18 November 1727, Sawai Jai Singh II founded Jaipur, the new capital city of the Kacchwaha dynasty, about 11 kilometres south of the old capital of Amber. Sawai Jai Singh was a scholar, statesman and a patron of the arts. A gifted Bengali engineer, Vidyadhar Chakravarty, helped build the city which was laid out according to the strict principles of town planning set down in the *Shilpa Shastra*—the ancient Hindu text of architecture. The royal residence was built at the centre of the new city.

Work began in 1727 on a grid plan that was tilted at an angle of 12 degrees east of north, to coincide with Leo, the astrological sign of the Kacchwaha dynasty, and took six years to complete. One of India's finest examples of a planned city, Jaipur or the 'The Pink City' is surrounded by a crenellated wall with seven massive arched gateways and has unusually wide intersecting streets which have created square urban blocks. A central north-south route leads up to the main entrance of the city palace, whereas the principal east-west thoroughfare is aligned with a shrine dedicated to Surya, the sun god.

The city palace complex has been the principal residence of the Kacchwahas since 1727. It is contained by high walls, and arched gateways on three sides provide access to the streets of the city bazaars. Sawai Jai Singh's famous astronomical observatory Jantar Mantar, built between 1728 and 1734, stands in the outer precinct of the complex.

Two gateways lead into the first inner courtyard, in the middle of which stands Mubarak Mahal, designed by the famous architect Samuel Swinton Jacob in the late 19th century.

THE DURBAR THRONES IN THE CITY PALACE, C. 1875.

*CHANDRA MAHAL AT NIGHTTIME. **FACING PAGE:** A PALACE RETAINER
IN ONE OF THE ROYAL HALLS AT THE CITY PALACE.*

The first floor of this sandstone palace has a fine display of royal costumes and textiles. Rajendra Pol—the gateway, also designed by Jacob—is flanked by arcades and guarded by two large marbles elephants on both sides. It leads to the second courtyard, where stands the original Diwan-i-Aam of Sawai Jai Singh, the Sarvataobhadra. Now a part of the museum, the hall has triple arcades on each side, with windows set in temple style frames, and with Mughal style arches painted around them.

Two gigantic silver urns, said to be the largest silver objects in world, are kept here. The urns were made to carry holy water from the river Ganga for Madho Singh II when he went to London to attend the coronation of Edward VII. The Diwan-i-Aam built later is an impressive formal ceremonial hall with cusped arches and European chandeliers. It now houses rare Rajput and Mughal miniature paintings, carpets, old manuscripts, palanquins and a silver throne.

Ganesh Pol, the gateway to the west, leads to the third inner court. Pritam Niwas Chowk or 'the court of the beloved' has four doorways representing the four seasons; delicately painted peacocks and lotus ferns adorn them. To the north lies the imposing seven-storey Chandra Mahal or the moon pavilion. Each floor is elaborately decorated. A marble channel at the ground level conducts water to a cascade in a

formal garden; the front of the ground level has a low-columned hall with cusped arches.

On the first level of the Chandra Niwas is the Subh Niwas, which was extensively remodeled in the 20th century to serve as a private dining hall and sitting area. Well appointed with silver objects, photographs, carpets and furniture, it has tiny peepholes in the painted windows at the upper level to allow the women of the royal household to observe the festivities.

On the fifth floor is the Chavi Niwas, with three exquisitely painted chambers in blue and white foliate patterns, originally intended for private receptions. The Chandra Mahal is crowned by a white marble pavilion with a Bangla roof at the top. Adjoining the Chandra Mahal to the west is the zenana.

Jai Niwas, the formal garden, is laid out in the Mughal charbagh style with a temple of Govind Deo erected by Sawai Jai Singh. The complex also has an impressive Sileh Khanna, the armoury, as well as a small shopping complex.

HAWA MAHAL

Just as the Taj Mahal represents Agra, Hawa Mahal, or the palace of breezes, is emblematic of Jaipur. Built in 1799 by Sawai Pratap Singh (r. 1778-1803), this structure is five storeys high but just one room deep. A baroque composition of projecting windows, and balconies with perforated screens, it was designed specially for the royal ladies to observe the bustling street life below. Dedicated to Lord Krishna, this lime and mortar structure can be climbed by a winding ramp. Within the complex are administrative offices and an archeological museum that has some utensils dating back to the 2nd century BC.

CITY PALACE

Udaipur

BUILT 1559 and later
LOCATION Udaipur, Rajasthan
BUILT BY Maharana Udai Singh
STYLE Rajput
DYNASTY Sisodia

Famous for its lakes and marble palaces, Udaipur was the capital city of the Sisodias, from where they ruled over Mewar. The Sisodias can trace their lineage back to AD 566 and ruled over Mewar for over 1,200 years, making them one of the oldest dynasties in the world. Founded by Maharana Udai Singh in 1559, Udaipur became the capital after the sacking of Chittorgarh in 1567 by the Mughals (see page 31).

The magnificent City Palace stretches along the shores of Lake Pichola, which was created by raising a dam between two hills. Dominating the cityscape of Udaipur, the City Palace complex includes many palaces; it has constantly been added to by the twenty-two maharanas who have ruled Mewar since the 16th century. Most of the palaces in the complex have now been converted into hotels or museums.

The main access to the complex, which is spread over five acres, is through the triple-arched Tripolia gate, constructed in 1713. Engraved at the top of the gate is the sun—the emblem of the Sisodia dynasty—flanked by Rajput and Bhil tribal warriors. Past the gate is the Manek Chowk with service apartments on either side of it. In the middle is a formal garden that was originally the parade ground.

The principle section of the palace, which lies beyond, actually consists of several palaces, most of which now form a part of the excellent City Palace Museum.

A succession of courtyards leads to the zenana, which originally was the mardana or the men's quarters. This is the oldest part of the palace, a solid

*THE SHEER WALLS OF THE CITY PALACE COMPLEX END IN A
CORNUCOPIA OF DECORATIVE ARCHES, DOMES AND TURRETS.*

block of apartments, with little ornamentation. This section houses the royal collection of paintings, armoury and costumes.

Beyond this is the Ganesh Pol, which leads into a courtyard decorated with frescoes and a marble relief of Lord Ganesh. The courtyard that follows is the Rajya Angan Chowk, enclosed on all sides by apartments. To its one side is the shrine of Dhuni Mata, the Kuldevi (family goddess) of the Sisodias.

The lovely Chandra Mahal, built in 1620, has beautiful lattice windows and images in marble relief adorning its walls. The Dilkhushal Mahal has murals depicting festivals and ceremonies. Built in 1620, it has two magnificent chambers—the Kanch Burj or the Glass Turret, which is decorated with red and silver glass inlay in the chevron pattern, and the Krishna Niwas, which now houses a superb collection of the Mewar miniature paintings. Legend has it that it was the apartment of the beautiful 16-year-old princess Krishna Kumari who committed suicide in 1807 when aspiring suitors from Jodhpur and Jaipur threatened to go to war over her hand.

Steps lead further up to the highest part of the complex, the Bari Mahal. The ornate Moti Mahal is said to be the palace of the controversial Maharana Jawan Singh (r. 1828-38), who nearly lost half his kingdom when he promised it to a dancing girl if she would walk on a tightrope across Lake Pichola. Alarmed advisors are said to have had the rope cut when she had reached midway and she drowned.

The Mor Chowk or the Peacock Court is so named after glass-mosaic peacocks which are modelled in high relief. Three more opulent palaces were built in the late-19th and early 20th century. Shiv Niwas Palace, Shambhu Niwas, the current residence of the descendants of the Udaipur rulers and Fateh Prakash Palace.

THE IMPOSING CITY PALACE COMPLEX, AS SEEN FROM LAKE PICHOLA.

DUNDLOD FORT

Dundlod

BUILT 1750
LOCATION Dundlod, Rajasthan
BUILT BY Thakur Keshri Singh
STYLE Rajput
DYNASTY Dundlod Thakurs

Dundlod lies in the heart of the Shekhawati region, 225 kilometres from Delhi. According to local legend, the town was originally called Shivgarh, but in the early 19th century, its name was changed to Dund in honour of the local deity, Dund Pal. This lead to its present name, Dundlod, or the abode of Dund Pal.

The arid Shekawati region, famous for its painted havelis, is tucked between the more prominent kingdoms of Jaipur and Bikaner. It is named after its famous 15th-century ruler Rao Shekha, who challenged the mighty Kacchwahas of Amber and wrested control of the region, though he was unable to establish a dominant kingdom.

In the 16th century, one of his descendants Raisalji, was granted the title of Raja by Akbar. Raisalji's sons consolidated the small kingdom and their descendants, in particular Shardul Singh, brought the towns of Jhunjhunu and Fatehpur under the Shekhawati control. The Shekhawats were again made subservient by Maharaja Sawai Jai Singh II and were given the status of 'Thakurs' by mid-17th century.

Dundlod gained prominence in 1750, when Thakur Kesri Singh, the youngest son of Thakur Shardul Singh, constructed a defensive fort there. Engaged in a number of onslaughts and battles with adjoining kingdoms and with the Mughals, the family regained its glory under Sheo Singh. Originally made to house the Thakur's private army, Dundlod Fort was converted into a luxurious residence by Sheo Singh in 1809, who, fearful for his life, sought refuge there after his father and brother were murdered.

Suraj Pol, the imposing gateway to the fort, leads to the Bichla Darwaza or the middle gate. Then comes the Uttar Pol, from where steps lead to the majestic Diwan Khana. Dating back to 1840, the Diwan Khana is furnished with European furniture and light fixtures. On the upper level lies the Duchatta, from which ladies watched the ceremonies below in purdah. The fort has an impressive library with a vast collection of books and manuscripts, mostly belonging to Rawal Harnath Singh (1905-76), a renowned scholar. In 1972, he had a section of the fort converted into a hotel.

FACING PAGE: THE MAIN DRAWING ROOM IN DUNDLOD FORT WITH GILT-WOOD FURNITURE.

JAIGARH

Jaipur

BUILT 1725
LOCATION Jaipur, Rajasthan
BUILT BY Sawai Man Singh &
Sawai Jai Singh II
STYLE Rajput
DYNASTY Kacchwaha

At the foothills of the Aravali range, approached through a pass, the spectacular hilltop fort of Jaigarh overlooks the old Kacchwaha capital of Amber. Work on Jaigarh or Victory Fort was begun by Man Singh I but it was completed by Sawai Jai Singh II in 1725 and is named after him. The fort is perched 400 feet above the Amber Fort, its perimeter walls over three kilometers long. A steep road leads to Dungar Darwaza, the massive entrance gateway.

The Jaigarh cannon foundry, built in the 16th century is one of the few surviving medieval foundries in the world. It has a furnace, lathe, tools and a collection of cannons. Jai Van, said to be the world's largest cannon, was cast here in 1726. It is said that this 50-tonne behemoth was test-fired only once and the cannon ball landed at a village 34 kilometres away! A battery of ten cannons faced the Delhi Road at the Damdama, an indication according to some that Man Singh was secretly preparing for a showdown with his Mughal allies.

The highest point in Jaigarh is the seven-storeyed Diya Burj with its panoramic view of the city of Jaipur. A huge oil lamp is lit here on the occasion of the king's birthday. Vijay Garh, the fort's armoury, has a large collection of swords and small arms, including a time bomb. Also on display are a treasury lock with five keys, and big wine and oil jars.

Besides the usual halls and chambers, the palace complex in the fort has a Khilbat Niwas (Commander's Meeting hall) in place of the Diwan-i-Khas (Hall of Private Audience). There is also the open pillared hall, Subhat Niwas. The Lakshmi Vilas palace inside the fort has some beautiful frescoes in blue and an old Mughal garden. There is a little 'theatre' hall for dance and music recital, and for puppet shows, which are still performed here.

The rainwater harvesting and water storage system of the fort are very impressive. There are three underground tanks and one of the reservoirs, Sagar Talav, has dams and octagonal bastions. The temples in the fort include the 10th century Shri Ram Hari Har Temple and the 12th century Kal Bhairava Temple.

FACING PAGE: BATTLEMENTS OF THE JAIGARH FORT STRETCH ALONG THE SPINE OF A HILL.

TREASURE HUNT

The well-defended Jaigarh fort served as the treasury of the Kachhwahas for a long time. Whenever Man Singh I (in the late 16th Century) or his successors fought and won gold, silver, jewels and other booty, they deposited it in the fort. The fort was guarded by the fiercely loyal Mina tribesmen. According to legend, so strictly did the Minas guard the treasury that they allowed each new Kachhwaha king to enter it only once and pick a single item for himself from the hoard!

All the treasure first paid for building Amber and then Jaipur, and for the lavish lifestyles of generations of royals. But persisting rumours of staggering amounts of hidden wealth actually induced the government of India to launch a massive treasure hunt at Jaigarh in 1976. The origin of this hunt actually goes to a *bijak* or a verse compilation under the possession of the family of Kripa Ram, a loyal minister of Sawai Jai Singh II. Supposedly, this *bijak* contained information about the amount of wealth and where it was hidden inside the fort. The three tanks at the southern end of the courtyard were actually drained, and other places dug and excavated in search of the elusive treasure. The futile search was called off after five long months. But it did have the beneficial consequence of rescuing Jaigarh from obscurity and putting it in its rightful place among India's great forts.

JAISALMER FORT
Jaisalmer

BUILT 1156
LOCATION Jaisalmer, Rajasthan
BUILT BY Rao Jaisal
STYLE Rajput
DYNASTY Bhati Rajput

Lying at the far edge of the Thar Desert, near the present-day border of India and Pakistan, Jaisalmer, India's Golden City, was founded when Rawal Jaisal began building a fort here in 1156. The fort was raised between 1156 and 1171 on the rocky ridge of Trikuta, surrounded by a vast, flat sandy expanse.

According to legend, after the great battle of Kurukshetra, Lord Krishna wandered around the desert with Arjun, where he prophesied that one day a descendant of his Yadav clan would establish a glorious desert kingdom around the Trikuta hill. A mendicant, Isa, narrated this story and its significance to Rawal Jaisal, who was on the lookout for a suitable site to build a fort that could be protected not only from his Bhati rivals, but also from the increasing menace of foreign invaders. Thus Jaisal Meru or 'rocky hill' came to be established.

Jaisalmer easily resolves into two cognate units, inseparable yet distinct and unique: the fort and the city. A bird's eye view reveals the fort as a glistening mound of gold. Seemingly crafted from a single block of stone, it is much larger than it first appears to be. Inside the fort, the cubical structures of palaces and dwellings contrast with the cylindrical bastions, segueing themselves in a piquant harmony.

An outer retaining wall built entirely with dry construction, without any binding material, circles the base of the Trikuta hill. The fort's structure kept evolving over long periods of time, particularly during the reigns of the maharawals (rulers) Bhim,

ALSO KNOWN AS SONAR QILA, JAISALMER'S FORT WAS BUILT IN THE 12TH CENTURY AND SERVED AS THE BASE OF THE BHATI RAJPUTS. WITH ITS 99 ROUNDED BASTIONS, THE FORT COMPLEMENTS ITS SANDY SURROUNDINGS.

Manmohan and Akhai Singh. A second wall was formed parallel to the legendary ninety-nine bastions and between this wall and the bastions is a pathway known in local parlance as mori. These bastions served as protective structures and lookout posts, and also served as homes to the guards. Placed strategically atop the wall are mammoth stone cannon balls which, when dropped from the height of the wall, could easily crush the enemy.

The entry to the fort is through a single gateway, the Akhai Pol. Three other gates—Suraj Pol, Ganesh Pol and, finally, Hawa Pol—have to be crossed before entering the main section of the fort. Hawa Pol accedes to Dussehra Chowk, a large open space with palaces on two sides and a beautiful Devi temple on the third. Slightly to the right of the chowk is a beautiful marble throne on a platform, placed at an angle to the side of the chowk, on which the maharawal sits to view the Dussehra celebrations. This throne also forms a part of the façade of the major palace complex known as Raja Ka Mahal, or the King's palace.

A large number of palaces are located along the sides of the Raja Ka Mahal, seemingly disassociated from one another yet linked cleverly by little corridors and stairways. Har Raj Ji Ka Mahal is the oldest palace and is assumed to have been built by Maharawal Har Raj in the 16th century. During recent restoration work, old stone inscriptions have been found that date sections of the palace to the 14th century. These stone inscriptions clearly specify the laying of the foundation stone of the palace as early as 1370 during Rawal Kehar's reign (r. 1361-1396). The palace is linked to another beautiful palace, the Sabha Niwas, also known as Moti Mahal, which was built by Maharawal Moolraj II in 1813. It is a three-storeyed building with a small garden laid out in Mughal fashion, complete with a fountain. Beautiful stone filigree work adorns the façade and the interiors, and one of the chambers inside

JAIN TEMPLES: REPOSITORIES OF LEARNING

The Jain temples inside the fort, built on the Solanki and Vaghela principles of Western Indian temple architecture, were built by wealthy Jain traders in the 15th and 16th centuries, a time when Jaisalmer was an important trading post. These temples house some rare works of art and ancient manuscripts which have been saved due to the Rajputs' commitment to protect their places of worship. In lieu of being allowed to build temples, the Maharawal often asked the traders to finance the building of the bastions in the fort, a request to which they necessarily had to accede. The Granth Bhandars in these temples preserve extremely rare collections of Jain manuscripts, most of which were brought from Gujarat. The complete collection comprises more than three thousand manuscripts, including five hundred palm-leaf manuscripts. The oldest and most important manuscript preserved here is the *Oghaniryukkti Vritti*, composed by Dronacharya in 1060. One of the oldest paper-leaf manuscripts, *Nyayarnartika Tarparya Tika* written by Vachaspati Mishra in 1222, is also part of the collection.

has scenes from the Raaslila—the play between Krishna, the divine cowherd, and gopis, his female friends—painted in fine detail and edged in gold.

The largest edifice inside the fort is the Raja Ka Mahal. It was probably first built by Maharawal Gaj Singh (1819-1846) and was added to subsequently. On both sides of the entrance to the palace are 'Jauhar' handprints of women who voluntarily immolated themselves as their men went out to die in battle. The complex contains apartments called Akhye Vilas, Gaj Vilas, Sarmohan Vilas and Rang Mahal. Built in 1884, Gaj Vilas represents the ubiquitous 19th-century craze for European lifestyles among the ruling elite. They came to adopt the trappings of a Western lifestyle, not just because of the political and social advantages that inevitably accrued to them, but also because of a genuine fondness for the unusual. This penchant is well illustrated in Gaj Vilas, with the blue-tiled room and the gilded mirror-work in the royal bedchamber giving a glimpse into the lifestyle of the Rajasthani royalty of the era.

Connected at two secret levels to Gaj Vilas is the Rani Ka Mahal or the Queen's Palace, a labyrinthine structure especially designed to make it near inaccessible to unwanted intruders. Curiously, the royal ladies did not have permanent rooms and would move from one set to another as seasons, festivals, religious celebrations and superstitions dictated.

Just opposite the Rani Ka Mahal is the Kunwar Pada, the Palace of the Princes. Sons of the royal family were moved to this palace when they turned twelve so that they may be close to their mothers and aunts, and be educated in statecraft, warfare, languages and religious lore. The Kunwar Pada has now, unfortunately, been stripped of its intricate stone façade to safeguard it from further damage. Extensive restoration work has been done in the fort by the Indian National Trust of Art and Cultural Heritage (INTACH).

PATWON KI HAVELI

The origins of the city of Jaisalmer can essentially be traced to the fort whence the population started to spill downwards to what is called the *talhatti*, around the 16th century. This created the nucleus around which the irregular polygon that is the city of Jaisalmer finally emerged. The city has the famous Patwon Ki Haveli, built as a group of five havelis (mansion), by a wealthy merchant, Guman Chand, who traded in gold and silver. These havelis were built for his five sons between 1800 and 1860. The opulence of the carvings on the stone facades is a testimony to the immense wealth of this family. Every inch of the façade of these six-storyed havelis is carved in fine detail and was obviously executed by the best gazdars (artisans who specialized in fitting together carved stones) and shilpis (master stone carvers) of the time. These havelis are said to be the most photographed structures in India, second only to the Taj Mahal.

CONSTRUCTED IN
INTERLOCKING
BLOCKS OF LOCAL
BUFF-COLOURED
SANDSTONE, THE
MASSIVE FORTRESS
SITS ATOP THE
TRIKUTA HILL.

JUNA MAHAL

Dungarpur

BUILT 14th century
LOCATION Dungarpur, Rajasthan
RESTORED BY Maharawal Shiv Singh
STYLE Rajput
DYNASTY Sisodia Rajput

Dungarpur is situated 130 kilometres from Udaipur in the extreme south of Rajasthan. The seven-storeyed palace of Juna Mahal was built in the 13th century when some members of the Sisodia dynasty of Mewar established a new kingdom here. The Mughal army captured it in 1573, however Dungarpur managed to retain its autonomy.

Juna Mahal is built on a large rock, at a height of 1,500 feet from sea level. The most well known ruler of Dungarpur was Maharawal Shiv Singh (r. 1730-85), who is credited with restoring the palace and adding new sections to it.

The top storey of the palace has a room containing a series of erotic paintings from the *Kama Sutra*, which probably served as the maharawal's bedroom. The palace walls and ceilings are covered with scenes from Dungarpur's history and the portraits of the erstwhile princes, dating from the 16th to the 18th century.

The richly decorated Durbar Hall and the Aam Khas served as the formal reception rooms of the palace. The Darbar Hall is painted completely in brilliant colours; prominently displayed are portraits of two maharanas of Udaipur—Shambhu Singh and Fateh Singh. Every inch of the Darbar Hall is painted—murals on the ceilings contrast with chevron patterned pillars and geometric patterns adorn one wall, while others depict hunting scenes. All combine to create an astonishing effect. Much of this was done in the latter half of the 19th century, during the reign of Maharawal Umed Singh II.

FACING PAGE: THE SEVEN-STOREYED PALACE WAS FIRST BUILT IN THE 13TH CENTURY. EXTENSIVE RESTORATION WAS DONE BY MAHARAWAL SHIV SINGH IN THE 18TH CENTURY.
FOLLOWING PAGES 56-57: THE JUNA MAHAL HAS A SERIES OF APARTMENTS EMBELLISHED WITH EXQUISITE INLAY WORK AND PAINTINGS.

JUNAGARH FORT

Bikaner

BUILT 1587-1593
LOCATION Bikaner, Rajasthan
BUILT BY Maharaja Rai Singh
STYLE Rajput
DYNASTY Rathore Rajput

Rao Bika, the younger son of Rao Jodha of Jodhpur, founded Bikaner in 1465. Knowing that he would never inherit the kingdom, Bika left with hundreds of followers and decided to settle at a new site on the sandy wastelands of northwest Rajasthan. He built a mud fort there and, along with Jodhpur and Jaisalmer, Bikaner became one of the prosperous states of the Thar desert. This was because of its strategic location on the caravan trade route to central Asia and China.

Bikaner became a model princely state under the reigns of Maharaja Dungar Singh (r. 1872-87) and Maharaja Ganga Singh (r. 1887- 1943). Maharaja Ganga Singh, one of the most progressive rulers of his time, brought water to his parched state by constructing a concrete canal that diverted water from the Sutlej river to Bikaner (see page 71). He also brought railways to Jodhpur, and built free hospitals and schools for his subjects.

Originally called Chintamani, the fort was constructed between 1587 and 1593 by Bikaner's third ruler, Rai Singh. This imposing citadel in the middle of Bikaner, which was never conquered, is protected by a 3,235-foot-long sandstone wall with thirty-seven bastions, a moat and the forbidding expanse of the Thar Desert.

Within the fort's strong impassive walls lie numerous palaces and pavilions and temples built over centuries by successive rulers. The Suraj Pol or the Sun Gate is the main entrance to the fort. Beyond it lie many courtyards that lead to the two large reception halls—Ganga Niwas and Vikram Vilas. A small inner

THE 16TH CENTURY CITADEL CONTAINS MANY PALACES, PAVILIONS AND TEMPLES BUILT OVER CENTURIES BY SUCCESSIVE RULERS.

THE THRONE ROOM OF
ANUP MAHAL INSIDE
THE JUNAGARH FORT.

courtyard leads to Anup Mahal, a sumptuously decorated 'hall of private audience' built by Maharaja Anup Singh in 1690, which was lavishly decorated by Maharaja Surat Singh between 1787 and 1800. The lime-plaster walls polished to a high sheen, covered with red and gold lacquer patterns, and interspersed with mirrors and gold-leaf work create a very beautiful effect.

Karan Mahal, the 'hall of public audience', which was built between 1631 and 1669, has a similar design though it is less extravagantly decorated. Two other heavily decorated and beautiful palaces are the 17th-century Chandra Mahal or the Moon Palace and the Phool Mahal, both built by Maharaja Gaj Singh in the 18th century.

Chandra Mahal has carved marble panels depicting the Radha-Krishna legend. There is a small silver bed in which Rao Bika is supposed to have slept with his feet touching the ground so that he could leap to his feet if surprised by an attacker! The walls of Badal Mahal or the Palace of Clouds have clouds painted on them,

providing visual relief in this dry, rain-parched land; there is a fresco of Krishna and Radha in the midst of rain clouds.

The Durbar Hall, which was built in the 20th century by Maharaja Ganga Singh, now houses the fort museum with its eclectic collection of armoury, including a 56 kg suit of armour, weapons and, among other things, a sandalwood throne said to belong to the ancestors of the Jodhpur royals who ruled over the ancient kingdom of Kanauj in the 5th century.

KUMBHALGARH FORT

Kumbhalgarh

BUILT 15th century
LOCATION Kumbhalgarh, Rajasthan
BUILT BY Rana Kumbha
STYLE Rajput
DYNASTY Sisodia

Known as the 'Eye of Mewar', the massive fortress of Kumbhalgarh is situated between Jodhpur and Udaipur in Rajasthan at a height of 3,445 feet. It was one of the most important fortresses of the maharanas of Mewar.

The fortress is named after Rana Kumbha of Chittorgarh, who built it in the 15th century. Kumbhalgarh was the most important defensive outpost in all of Rajasthan, justly renowned as the most difficult fort to conquer. According to local legend, it was conquered only once in its entire history and that too because its water supply was poisoned. Its massive perimeter wall spans an astounding 36 kilometres and its wide ramparts could accommodate six horsemen riding abreast. The path to its entrance had seven fortified spiked gates—the spikes meant to deter elephants from beating them down.

The massive walls of the fort contain a number of palaces, monuments and temples, which were built over the next few centuries. Kumbhalgarh actually has another fort within its walls—the Kartargarh fort. This inner fort has a palace, which was built by Maharana Fateh Singh

THE IMPREGNABLE 'EYE OF MEWAR', SAID TO HAVE BEEN CONQUERED ONLY ONCE IN ITS ENTIRE HISTORY.

after he had pulled down the old palace built by Rana Kumbha

No palace or structure survives from the time of Rana Kumbha. A small 19th-century palace, Badal Mahal, crowns the summit of this mountain stronghold, its chambers painted in pink, green and turquoise. The Fatehprakash palace upstairs has a durbar hall decorated with lime plaster and paintings, a zenana covered with paintings of flora and fauna, and a Ganesh temple in the courtyard. Also noteworthy are the ventilation systems of the toilets and the chimney systems of the kitchen complex.

It was at Kumbhalgarh that the infant Maharana Udai Singh, the future builder of Udaipur, was brought for safety after there was an attempt on his life in 1536. Kumbhalgarh was also the birthplace of Maharana Pratap (1540-97), a descendant of Rana Kumbha. Rana Pratap's name is forever etched in Indian history as the brave warrior who took on the might of the Mughal emperor Akbar.

The Navachoki Mandeva temple inside the fort is dedicated to Lord Shiva and has a large shivlinga (iconic representation of Shiva). The temple has black granite slabs with Mewar's history inscribed on them, the earliest slab dating back to 1491. Maharana Kumbha's cenotaph is next to this temple.

BUILT ATOP A STRATEGIC PASS IN THE FORESTS OF THE ARAVALI HILLS, KUMBHALGARH OFFERS A CLEAR VIEW OF THE VAST EXPANSE OF THE COUNTRYSIDE FOR MILES AROUND IT.

THE LAKE PALACE: THE SON'S ANSWER WHEN HE WAS NOT
ALLOWED TO USE FATHER'S PLEASURE PALACE.
FOLLOWING PAGES 66-67: THE CITY PALACE COMPLEX PROVIDES
AN IMPOSING BACKDROP TO THE PRISTINE-WHITE LAKE PALACE
IN THE PLACID BLUE WATERS OF LAKE PICHOLA.

LAKE PALACE

Udaipur

BUILT 1746
LOCATION Udaipur, Rajasthan
BUILT BY Rana Jagat Singh II
STYLE Rajput
DYNASTY Sisodia

Situated on an island in the middle of Lake Pichola in Udaipur, Jag Niwas, better known as the Lake Palace, is among the most scenic and romantically situated palaces in the world and it is now among the better-known luxury hotels in the world as well.

Udaipur was the seat of the Sisodias, from where they ruled over Mewar, and for over a hundred years Jag Niwas served as their main pleasure palace and summer retreat. It is said that during the rule of Maharana Sangram Singh II (r. 1716-34), his son Jagat Singh wanted to spend time at Jag Mandir, the palace situated on an island at the southern end of Lake Pichola. Permission was not granted to the young prince and instead he was given the adjacent island on the lake. Pavilions were built before 1734 and when Maharana Jagat Singh II (r. 1734-51) ascended the throne, he further expanded the palace, naming it Jag Niwas after himself. The marble water palace took three years to build and was inaugurated with much fanfare in January 1746, the festivities lasting for three days.

During the reign of Jagat Singh, the Bara Mahal, Dhola Mahal, Dilaram Palace and Phool Mahal, all were added to the Lake Palace. The Khush Mahal (Palace of Happiness) is now called the Maharani Suite as it used to be the queens' residence. With marble floors and coloured-glass windows, it is a perfect place to watch the sun set. There is also the Kamal Mahal, with beautiful glass-inlay work and the Udai Prakash which has a large open terrace. With picturesque balconies and many gardens with fountains, it was an ideal setting for boating parties, musical evenings and other leisure activities.

However, by the latter half of the 19th century, time and weather were taking their toll and Jag Niwas was steadily sliding into a dilapidated state. When Maharana Bhagawat Singh ascended the throne in 1955, he decided that the only way to preserve Jag Niwas's heritage was to convert it into Udaipur's first luxury hotel.

It was extensively restored in 1955, its pavilions were enlarged, and its ponds and gardens were cleaned and repaved. It opened in 1963 as a luxury hotel and became immensely popular with celebrities, and film producers and directors. The Lake Palace Hotel has had many distinguished guest, including Queen Elizabeth II and the Duke of Edinburgh, Jacqueline Kennedy, the Shah of Iran and the king of Nepal.

LALLGARH PALACE

Bikaner

BUILT 1901-1926
LOCATION Bikaner, Rajasthan
BUILT BY Maharaja Ganga Singh
STYLE Rajput
DYNASTY Rathore Rajput

Maharaja Ganga Singh of Bikaner built the Lallgarh Palace towards the end of the 19th century in memory of his father Maharaja Lall Singh. It was designed by the renowned architect Sir Samuel Swinton Jacob in his perfected Indo-Saracenic style. The entire complex is laid out in a sprawling compound outside the walled town. Maharaja Ganga Singh moved here as a young man and continued to live here.

The initial budget for building the palace was a 'modest' one lakh rupees (Rs 1,00,000). There was even talk of reducing costs further. But then the maharaja got personally involved in the building exercise and all talk of budgets and cost cutting was dismissed. Work on the palace began in 1896; by the time Laxmi Niwas, one of the four sections was completed in 1902, costs had already escalated by ten times to ten lakh rupees (Rs 10,00,000). Intricate stone carvings replaced cheap stucco and the palace was ready just in time to host Lord Curzon as its first important guest.

The Indo-Saracenic architecture of the palace is a blend of the traditional Rajput and European styles. It can be seen in the exquisite jalis, jharokas and arches in the traditional Rajput style, all made from locally available red sandstone. Richly carved fire mantles, Italian colonnades and interiors furnished with Belgian chandeliers, cut glass ornaments, oil paintings and antique lamps reflect the European influence.

The palace is built around two interior courtyards that provide access to the public and private zones. One of the most beautiful rooms in Lallgarh is the Swarna Mahal, decorated in the mixed European-Rajput style. Elegant woodwork blends with painted frescoes and delicate gold-leaf work covers the walls and ceilings.

The royal family continues to live in the palace, a part of which now runs as two independent hotels and a section houses the Maharaja Sadul museum which displays vintage photographs and other artefacts.

THE FAÇADE OF THIS IMPOSING TURN-OF-THE-CENTURY MONUMENT IS INDIAN, WHILE THE INTERIORS ARE WESTERN, THE CROSS-CULTURAL BLEND BEING SURPRISINGLY SUCCESSFUL.

MAHARAJA GANGA SINGH

Maharaja Ganga Singh of Bikaner (r. 1887 - 1943) was among the most dynamic princely rulers of India. Not only did he build the imposing Lallgarh palace, he was also instrumental in the economic development of Bikaner. He brought railways to his state, and by 1935, a railway network of 1,000 miles was laid out across the Bikaner state. He was also the architect of the Ganga canal, an ambitious irrigation project that turned vast tracts of desert into rich farmland. But Sir Ganga Singh (he was knighted by the British) is perhaps best known for his spectacular grouse shoots, to which every one from the British Viceroy down vied to be invited. The maharaja realized the scope for diplomacy that these occasions provided and his guests included the Prince of Wales (later King George V) and George Clemenceau, the president of France. Ganga Singh later lead the Indian delegation to the League of Nations.

PAGES 70-71: THE LALLGARH BAND PLAYS OUTSIDE THE PALACE.

AN UNDATED OLD IMAGE OF A HOLI PROCESSION, COMPLETE WITH
ELEPHANT AND HOWDAH, PASSING THE FORT IN BHARATPUR. HOLI,
THE FESTIVAL OF COLOURS, IS ACCOMPANIED BY MUCH REVELRY
AND CELEBRATED WITH GUSTO.

LOHAGARH

Bharatpur

BUILT 18th century
LOCATION Bharatpur, Rajasthan
BUILT BY Raja Suraj Mal
STYLE Mughal
DYNASTY Jat Dynasty

The kingdom of Bharatpur was founded by the Jats who, along with the Dholpurs, were the only non-Rajputs to have ruled in Rajasthan. Originally landowners, they claim descent from the Jadons of Bayana, a fortified town 45 kilometres southwest of Bharatpur.

The Mughal emperor Farrukh Siyar granted the Jat chieftains of the region titles and lands in 1714 in a bid to buy peace. Their most remarkable leader, Raja Suraj Mal (r. 1724-63), fortified the city of Bharatpur in 1733 and used the Mughal loot to decorate the forts and palaces of his kingdom. In 1761, he captured Agra after defeating the Maratha forces. His son, Maharaja Jawahar Singh (r. 1763-82) temporarily established the Jat headquarters at the Red Fort in Agra.

At the centre of Bharatpur is Lohagarh or the Iron Fort, which served as the headquarters of the Jat kingdom of Bharatpur from the mid-18th century on. The fort has strong stone-lined double ramparts and is surrounded by a deep moat. Both the Marathas and the British were unable to conquer it in the 18th century, till it was captured by Lord Lake in 1805. In 1818, Bharatpur became the region's first princely state to sign a treaty with the East India Company.

Within the ramparts lies a lovely Mughal-style palace, which has three graceful pavilions with bangla roofs and arcaded verandahs arranged around a pleasure garden. The oldest of these pavilions is Badan Mahal, which was built by Badan Singh, the first ruler of Bharatpur.

Maharaja Balwant Singh built the Khas Mahal in the mid 19th-century; the spectacular hammam (bath) in this pavilion has a painted roof with a hole in it for the steam to escape and its floor is decorated with elaborate multi-colour stonework. Khas Mahal served as the royal residence and its craftsmanship testifies to the wealth of the rulers of Bharatpur.

Two of the pavilions now house the state museum, which has a rare collection of stone carvings dating back to the 1st and 2nd century AD. Sometime in the early 20th century, Maharaja Kishan Singh shifted the royal residence from Lohagarh to Moti Mahal, a new palace built in a revived Rajput-Mughal style.

The palace has an elegant arcaded loggia (an open sided gallery) that serves as the entrance porch. Intricate stonework and beautiful perforated jalli screens are proof of Kishan Singh's refined aesthetics.

THE SIX-STOREYED TOWER IN BADAL MAHAL, SHAPED LIKE A TAZIA,
WAS A GIFT BY THE MUSLIM CRAFTSMEN AS A MARK OF THEIR LOVE
AND RESPECT FOR THE ROYAL FAMILY OF JAISALMER.

MANDIR PALACE

Jaisalmer

LOCATION Jaisalmer, Rajasthan
BUILT BY Maharawal Jawahar Singh
STYLE Rajput
DYNASTY Bhati Rajput

Legend proclaims that the maharawals of Jaisalmer moved their residence from the Jaisalmer Fort down to the city because of a curse that no son would be born to them in the fort. For seven generations they did not have a son and so they moved out of the fort during the reign of Maharawal Jawahar Singh. Astoundingly, as soon as they moved to Mandir Palace, a son was born to the maharawal and the direct line of descent continues till today. The Mandir Palace complex has two palaces and seventeen temples, most of which are open to the public. The older of the two main palaces, Badal Vilas, built by Maharawal Berisal, has a six-storeyed tower, shaped like a tazia (a ceremonial replica of a tomb of Imam Hussain, revered by Shia Muslims). It was a gift by the Muslim craftsmen as a mark of their love and respect for the royal family.

The royal insignia of Jaisalmer is beautifully carved on the stone façade of the palace. The royal family continues to stay here, though part of it has been converted into a hotel. The palace comes alive during festivals like Holi and Dussehra, when the local people join the royal family in celebrations.

Jaisalmer has a couple of beautiful garden palaces a little away from the city. Mool Sagar is a garden palace built by Rawal Mool Raj II. Set amidst gardens, this romantic palace has a painted room, delicately carved chattris and Jaisalmer's largest carved jharokha on the rooftop. An old step-well still waters the lemon orchards surrounding it.

The garden palace of Amar Sagar was built by Maharawal Amar Singh in 1692. Laid out on the edge of the Amar Sagar lake, it has beautiful views of Jain temples across on the other side. Old trees, a small kund (water tank) and a water pavilion that gets encircled with gently lapping waves during the monsoons lend the place a unique atmosphere.

MEHRANGARH FORT

Jodhpur

BUILT 1459
LOCATION Jodhpur, Rajasthan
BUILT BY Rao Jodha Singh
STYLE Rajput
DYNASTY Rathore Rajput

IN the mid-15th century, the Rathore Rajputs established their rule over Marwar, a vast expanse of the Thar Desert in western Rajasthan. Rao Jodha (r. 1438-88) founded Jodhpur in 1459 and built the Mehrangarh Fort on a hill overlooking the city. It was from here that his descendants ruled over the largest of the Rajput kingdoms.

The most majestic of the forts of Rajasthan, described as, 'the creation of angels, fairies and giants' by Rudyard Kipling, the Mehrangarh Fort rises sheer out of a 410-foot-high hill originally known as Bhakucheeria or the Mountain of Birds.

Legend has it that when Rao Jodha chose this hill as the site for his citadel in the 15th century, the only human inhabitant here was an old man, Cheria Nathji or the lord of the birds. Angry at Rao Jodha, he cursed him, 'May your kingdom never have water!' To placate him, Rao Jodha built a house for him in the new city of Jodhpur and a temple around his cave on the hill. Both the cave and the temple still exist.

The high-flying cheels (pariah kites), sacred to the Rathores, still circle the fort and are represented in the Jodhpur coat of arms. Succeeding generations of the Rathore rulers expanded and embellished the fort that Jodha built.

Parts of the bastioned walls are hewn out of the rock itself and, in places, are more than 24 metre thick and 40 metre high. Perched on them are old cannons. The palace inside is a blend of myriad styles and influences, and is mostly assigned to the reigns of Jaswant Singh I and Ajit Singh in the latter half of the 17th century. The palace is approached by a circuitous path with seven arched gateways, the first being Fateh Pol or Victory Gate and the last being Loha Pol or Lion Gate. Outside the Loha Pol is a wall with the handprints of satis— women who immolated themselves as their husbands rode off to fight till death.

The most opulent chamber in the fort is the Phool Mahal which was built between 1730 and 1750. Richly painted, it was used for royal celebrations. Placed here was the gold-plated royal throne, with a ceremonial umbrella behind it. The heavily ornamented Takhat Vilas was the favorite retreat of Maharaja Takhat Singh (r. 1843-73), who is said to have had thirty queens and

FACING PAGE: 'THE CREATION OF ANGELS, FAIRIES AND GIANTS', MEHRANGARH SEEMS TO RISE OUT OF THE BHAKUCHEERIA HILL.

SACRIFICE AT MEHRANGARH

The foundation of the Mehrangarh fort was laid on 12 May 1459. It is said that Jodha took the extreme step of burying a man, named Rajya Bambi, alive in the foundation of the fort to ensure that the new site proved propitious. Even today Rajiya's descendants share a special relationship with the present maharaja of Jodhpur and reside in Raj Bagh or Rajiya's Garden, the estate bequeathed to their ancestor by Jodha.

While Rajiya's sacrifice is an established fact, according to less reliable accounts there were three other human burials in the fort's foundations, taking the tally to four—one on each of the fort's four corners. Among the buried, according to these accounts, was a Brahmin named Mehran and the fort was named Mehrangarh or Mehran's fort after him. Chances are, though, that the story is apocryphal; *mehr* is the Rajasthani word for sun and, in all probability, the Rathores, who claim descent from the sun, named the fort after the sun.

many concubines. The room is brightly painted with murals of Radha, Krishna and the gopis.

Moti Mahal, the hall of private audience, built between 1581 and 1595, has a gorgeous ceiling decorated with mirrors and gold leaf. Crushed seashells mixed with plaster give the walls a high sheen. The Jhanki Mahal on the uppermost level has a long gallery with exquisite latticed-stone screens. The royal ladies watched the official proceedings in the courtyard below from here. Today, it houses a rich collection of royal cradles. The cradles are decorated with gilt mirrors, and figures of fairies, elephants and birds.

The Shringar Chowk has the white-marble coronation throne of the Jodhpur rulers. Every ruler after Rao Jodha has been crowned on it. The zenana has hundreds of intricate jalis on the façade and is constructed around a big chowk, the Daulat Khana Chowk.

All the apartments now form a part of the museum, displaying a fascinating collection of, among other things, weapons, miniature paintings, portraits and sculptures. The Palanquin Gallery and the Howdah Gallery display many fine specimens, including a silver howdah that was gifted by Emperor Shah Jahan in 1653.

Restoration work on the fort was started by Maharaja Gaj Singh II in the early 1970s under his private trust, the Mehrangarh Museum Trust, and much has been restored since. Currently, Chokelao Palace, a pleasure palace built around a sunken garden is being restored. The Mehrangarh Fort is among the more commendable examples of restoration and preservation of India's heritage.

NAGAUR FORT

Nagaur

BUILT 12th century
LOCATION Nagaur, Rajasthan
STYLE Rajput
DYNASTY Chauhan/Delhi
Sultans/Mughal/Rathore

Strategically placed between Jodhpur and Bikaner, the small desert town of Nagaur is dominated by Ahhichatragarh Fort, also known as the Nagaur Fort.

The fort once linked the old trade routes from Sindh, Kabul and Multan to Gujarat and the Gangetic plains. At first a mud fort constructed as early as the 4th century, the Ahhichatragarh Fort was rebuilt in stone in the 12th century.

The circular fort was originally occupied by the Chauhan Rajputs, one of the oldest Rajput clans of Rajasthan. It was then occupied by the Delhi sultans and the Mughal emperor Akbar, who used it as his principal headquarters in Rajasthan.

In the 18th century, the ruler of Jodhpur, Maharaja Abhai Singh, received the fort as a gift from the Mughals. In 1725, Abhai Singh presented the fort to his brother Bhakta Singh, who had helped him gain the Rathore throne by murdering their father Ajit Singh. Bhakta Singh resided in the fort until his death in 1752. He embellished it with a charming pleasure palace, and built an ingenious system to transport water and a system of air-ducts that used to supply the inner-rooms with cool air.

The main terrace of the palace has a beautiful ninety-nine-pillared pavilion to its right and the multi-storey Hadi Rani Mahal to its left. Delicate Persian-style winged angels are painted on the ceiling of the apartments in the Hadi Rani Mahal. Abha Mahal, a private reception hall at the centre of the complex, has a big hammam or bathing room that has a dome with an opening at the top. Another pavilion, Akbari Mahal, is painted with murals of cloud-borne courtiers and maidens.

Water, so precious in the desert, was meticulously collected in traditional step-wells and tanks, and carried to every corner of the fort through a network of waterways. This intricate system filtered and recycled water from one pool to another, bringing life to the gardens and forming a sparkling trail through the palaces. Nagaur Fort is being restored by the Mehrangarh Musuem Trust and has recently received the UNESCO Heritage Award for the outstanding restoration work being done there.

FACING PAGE: AERIAL VIEW OF THE PALACES AND GARDENS INSIDE AHHICHATRAGARH FORT.

INDIAN ROYALTY IS KNOWN FOR THEIR EQUESTRIAN PROWESS AND
SOME OF THE GLAMOUR OF THE ROYAL POLO MATCHES IS ON
DISPLAY IN THE POLO BAR AT THE RAMBAGH PALACE.

RAMBAGH PALACE

Jaipur

BUILT 1835
LOCATION Jaipur, Rajasthan
STYLE Rajput
DYNASTY Kacchwaha

Situated just outside of Jaipur's old walled city, the Rambagh Palace was built in 1835 on a modest scale for the queen's favourite handmaiden. It was later refurbished as a royal guesthouse and a hunting lodge in 1887 during the reign of Maharaja Sawai Madho Singh, who added tennis and squash courts, an indoor swimming pool and a polo field.

In 1933 it became the official residence of Madho Singh's adopted heir, Man Singh II, who hired Hammonds of London to redo the interiors, and lived here with his wife Maharani Gayatri Devi after their marriage in 1940. New additions included an exotic Chinese room in red and gold; black marble bathrooms; Lalique crystal chandeliers and an illuminated dining table.

The Rambagh is an architectural masterpiece, its colonnaded corridors with potted palms, marble courtyards and fretted screens reflecting a blend of Rajput and Mughal styles. Overlooking courtyards with fountains, the rooms open out onto airy verandahs and offer views of vast lawns dotted with mango trees.

In 1957, Man Singh moved to the smaller Raj Mahal Palace and Rambagh Palace opened as a luxury hotel. The palace has beautiful neo-classical elements like the indoor pool set amidst intricate fretted screens and stained-glass panels.

FOLLOWING PAGES 86-87: MAHARAJA MAN SINGH II, WHO WAS ELEVEN YEARS OLD WHEN HE ASCENDED TO THE THRONE, WAS SENT TO LIVE AT RAMBAGH A SAFE DISTANCE AWAY FROM THE INTRIGUES OF THE ZENANA. HE LIVED THERE WITH HIS THREE MAHARANIS AND FIVE CHILDREN TILL THE PALACE WAS CONVERTED INTO A LUXURY HOTEL.

SAMODE PALACE
Samode

BUILT 19th century
LOCATION Jaipur, Rajasthan
BUILT BY Rawal Bairi Sal
STYLE Rajput
DYNASTY Nathawat Rawals

Tucked away in the rugged Aravali Hills, 40 kilometres north of Jaipur is the beautiful Samode Palace. Its simple exterior belies the beauty found inside.

Still home to the Nathawat Rawals, the complex dates mainly from the time of Rawal Bairi Sal and Rawal Sheo Singh, both of whom served as prime ministers under Sawai Jai Singh III and his successor Sawai Ram Singh II, the Kacchwaha rulers of Jaipur in the 19th century. It was Rawal Bairi Sal who signed the historic treaty on behalf of Maharaja Sawai Jagat Singh that made Jaipur a protectorate of the East India Company in 1818. The family traces their origins to when Amber used to be the Kacchwaha capital.

A winding road leads up to the living quarters of the palace, built along a series of courtyards. The beautiful murals and mirror-work interiors have been painstakingly restored and the palace is now run as a hotel. The zenana, which is more beautifully decorated than the Sultan Mahal or the mardana (men's quarters), comes as a pleasant surprise. The Durbar Hall is a riot of colours, with Mughal-style miniature paintings embedded in the walls, and niches with flowery patterns, which cover the walls and the ceiling. The terraced gardens some distance away are used for outdoor dinners.

BUILT IN THE LATE-NINETEENTH CENTURY, SAMODE PALACE HAS BEEN USED AS A LOCATION FOR ROMANTIC HOLLYWOOD FILMS.
FOLLOWING PAGES 90-91: *SWIRLING KALBELIYA DANCERS IN THE ORNATE DURBAR HALL AT THE SAMODE PALACE.*

FINE CRAFTS=
MANSHIP AT
THE SAMODE
PALACE.

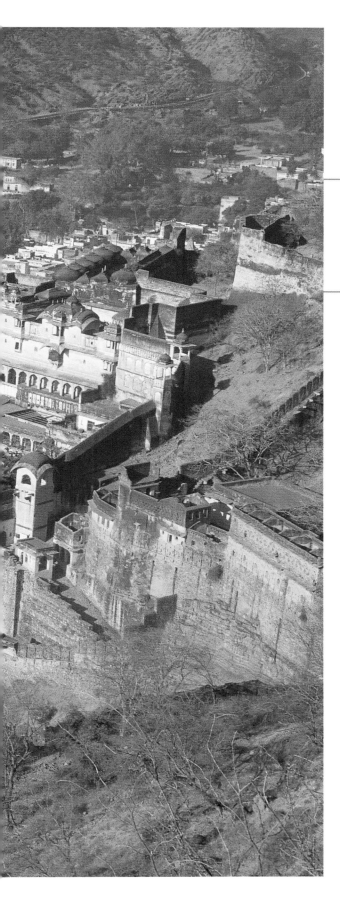

TARAGARH FORT

Bundi

BUILT 16th century
LOCATION Bundi, Rajasthan
BUILT BY Rao Surtan Singh
& successors
STYLE Rajput
DYNASTY Hada Chauhan clan

Nestled amongst the Aravali hills in south Rajasthan lies the small state of Bundi, the undiscovered jewel of Rajasthan. Founded in 1341 by Rao Deva, chief of the 'fire-born' Hada Chauhan clan, Bundi had a love-hate relationship with the more powerful state of Mewar. Along with intermarriages, there were constant skirmishes between the two states. Peace and prosperity came with acceptance of Mughal suzerainty, when Rao Surjan Singh (r. 1554-85) curried favour with the Mughal emperor Akbar, after surrendering the Ranthambore fort that he was manning for the Sisodias of Mewar.

The garh-palace of Taragarh, a citadel at the top of a 500-foot-high hill, is described by Col. James Todd, in his definitive work, *Annals and Antiquities of Rajasthan*, as, 'the coup d'oeil of the castellated palace of Boondi, from whichever side you approach it, is the most striking in India.'

Work on the main palace, situated below, began in the 16th century, and it was added to over the next 200 years at different levels of the hillside. Instead of sandstone, the favoured construction material of the Rajput kings, the palace is made from the locally quarried, hard stone that does not lend itself easily to carving. Perhaps this is the reason why that the palace is decorated with the finest wall paintings found in Rajasthan.

The palace is protected by two fortification wall—its own thick,

THE CHATTAR MAHAL PALACE AS SEEN FROM TARAGARH FORT ABOVE. THE PALACE LOOKS LIKE AN EXTENSION OF THE HILLSIDE.

high and sheer walls, and also by an outer fortification wall linked to Taragarh. A paved ramp between this outer wall and the palace leads to the Hathian Pol or Elephant Gate, flanked by two slender but strong octagonal gates which are topped by a pair of huge painted elephants forming an arch. Elephants are an especially favourite motif in Bundi, though they are found in other Rajput palaces as well.

The most spectacular sections are the Chattar Mahal, built by Maharao Chatra Sal (r. 1631-58) in 1660, and the Chitra Shala, built between 1748 and 1770. Chatra Sal's private apartments consist of a suite of three chambers: a central, long chamber flanked by two small square ones. The walls of the central chamber have pegs, modelled like elephants and horses, and between these pegs are niches to keep objects. Murals cover the walls of the sourthern chambers, depicting the festival of Dussehra and palace life. The Chitra Shala overlooks a hanging garden, and the murals here are of the finest quality that can be found in Rajput palaces. The most spectacular of these is a series depicting Krishna with Radha and his gopis.

THE SCENES AT CHITRA SHALA, COMMISSIONED BY UMED SINGH IN THE 18TH CENTURY, DEPICT RAS LEELA (LORD KRISHNA'S DIVINE PLAY) AND COURT LIFE.

UMAID BHAWAN PALACE

Jodhpur

BUILT 1925
LOCATION Jodhpur, Rajasthan
BUILT BY Maharaja Umaid Singh
STYLE Art Deco
DYNASTY Rathore Rajput

The awe-inspiring Umaid Bhawan Palace, built on a monumental scale in creamy-pink sandstone, was commissioned in 1925 by Maharaja Umaid Singh of Jodhpur. Work on the palace, which was conceived as a famine relief-work project, began in 1929 and it took 3,000 men and fifteen years to complete, in the process providing welcome employment to Jodhpur's subjects. Nineteen kilometres of railway track were laid to bring the sandstone from the quarry to the building site.

Henry Vaughn Lanchester, the renowned Edwardian-era architect, designed this palace in the fashionable art deco style of the time. Umaid Bhawan was to become the last of the great palaces of India and the biggest private residence in the world. Built on the grandest possible scale, the palace has an imposing façade that is punctuated by towers and topped by a dome rising 56 metres above the central rotunda, with the residential wings fanning out in a symmetrical fashion.

A prime example of the opulent lifestyles of India's maharajas, the palace has 374 rooms, eight dining halls, two theatres, lavishly decorated reception halls and a big underground swimming pool. As part of the festivities during the inauguration of the palace, a glittering sit-down dinner for a 1,000 people was held in the dining

UMAID BHAWAN: THE LAST OF THE GREAT PALACES OF INDIA AND THE BIGGEST PRIVATE RESIDENCE IN THE WORLD.

hall. The central rotunda is reached after passing through a reception hall with the ballroom and banquet hall on either side. There is the Throne Room with its exquisite murals from the epic Ramayana, an elegant wood-panelled library, and even a private museum. Sports facilities include a billiards room, tennis courts, and unique marble squash courts. The palace museum has an impressive display of weapons and an incredible collection of clocks. Of special interest is a huge banner, which was presented by Queen Victoria.

Maharaja Gaj Singh, Umaid Singh's grandson, continues to live in a section of the palace, and a part of it now runs as a luxury hotel. The private section has beautiful, original art deco furniture, as well as paintings on themes from Hindu mythology done by the self-exiled Polish artist, Julius Stefan Norblin.

RATHORES OF JODHPUR

Jodhpur was the capital of Marwar, now a part of the state of Rajasthan. Marwar has had a turbulent history, where extended periods of war and strife were interspersed with periods of calm. The Rathore rulers of Marwar were constantly warring with the Mughals, and with their neighbours. However, peace reigned during the rule of Raja Udai Singh (r. 1581-95), after he formally acknowledged Akbar's sovereignty in 1583 and married his daughter to Akbar's son, prince Salim who later became Emperor Jehangir. The reign of Aurangzeb in Delhi, in the latter half of the 17th century, saw the occupation of Marwar by the Mughal forces.

Another period of relative calm came after Maharaja Ajit Singh (r. 1707-24) recaptured Jodhpur and married his daughter to Emperor Farukh Siyar. In 1839, during the reign of Maharaja Man Singh (1803-43), Jodhpur was forced to accept the presence of a British resident. Many judicial, educational and social reforms were introduced during the rule of Maharaja Takhat Singh (r. 1843-73) and Jodhpur emerged as a prosperous and modern state. He was succeeded by Maharaja Jaswant Singh II (r. 1873-95). During his rule Sir Pratap Singh was the Prime Minister. Pratap Singh is credited with bringing the first Indian polo team to England. The special riding breeches known as 'Jodhpurs' became popular all over the world after this event.

Maharaja Jaswant Singh II was succeeded by Maharaja Umaid Singh (r. 1918-47), whose famine relief policy led to the building of the spectacular Umaid Bhawan Palace and a dam that still works as Jodhpur's main source of water.

After Independence, Jodhpur was assimilated in the new state of Rajasthan during the reign of the dynamic Hanwant Singh (r. 1947-52), who died in an air crash while flying his plane. His four-year-old son assumed the title of Maharaja Gaj Singh II. Affectionately known as Bapji, he has worked tirelessly towards the promotion and preservation of Jodhpur's cultural and architectural legacy.

MAHARAJA GAJ SINGH II WITH HIS FAMILY IN FORMAL ATTIRE AGAINST THE BACKDROP OF UMAID BHAWAN.
FOLLOWING PAGE 104-105: *THE WHITE MARBLE BARADARI IN THE LAWNS BEHIND UMAID BHAWAN PALACE. ITS PRISTINE WHITE IS SET OFF TO PERFECTION BY THE MULTI-COLOURED BLAZE OF BOUGAINVILLEAS IN FULL BLOOM.*

VINAY VILAS PALACE

Alwar

BUILT 1793
LOCATION Alwar, Rajasthan
BUILT BY Maharaja Bakhtawar Singh
STYLE Rajput
DYNASTY Kacchwaha (Naruka clan)

Pratap Singh (1753-91) a courageous soldier. who earned fame for defending the Ranthambore Fort from the Marathas and helping the Kachhawahas of Jaipur against the Jats was rewarded with several estates to the east of Jaipur. By 1775, he had succeeded in ousting the Jats from the Alwar Fort, which then became the headquarters of his state. His son, Maharaja Bakhtawar Singh (1791-1815), added to their territories by collaborating with Lord Lake in the British campaign of 1803 against the Marathas, thus further strengthening Alwar.

Vinay Vilas Palace, also known as City Palace, was built in 1793 during the reign of Maharaja Bakhtawar Singh. In the 19th century, however, it was considerably expanded by Maharaja Vinay Singh, after whom the complex is now named.

Located beneath a hill, the palace, with its extravagant architectural features, testifies to the wealth of its builders. The central courtyard with its lovely marble pavilions opens to the lavishly decorated Durbar Hall, wherein lies a gilded marble throne under an ornamental bangla vault. The zenana, located in a separate wing with its own entrance, has private apartments built on three levels.

The palace is no longer used as a royal residence and a door to the right leads to the City Palace Museum

that holds many treasures, including rare, exquisite copies of the *Gulistan* written in 1258 by the Persian poet Sa'adi and the *Baburnama*, the memoirs of the Mughal emperor Babur. The museum has an excellent collection of Mughal and Rajput miniature paintings on display, along with arms and royal regalia. The rest of the complex houses the offices of the District Collectorate.

Behind the palace, across the grand *kund* (stepped tank), lie the spectacular chattris of Maharaja Bakhtawar Singh and his wife, Rani Musi. The Rani's cenotaph is a brown sandstone and white marble monument, and has a central chamber with a ceiling adorned with gold-leaf paintings portraying scenes from Krishna's life.

On the hill above is the 10th-century fort, Bala Qila or Alwar Fort. It was originally a mud fort and, later, the Mughals and the Jats extensively added to it before it was captured by Pratap Singh. The massive ramparts of the fort offer a spectacular view of the city.

BUILT IN THE 18TH CENTURY, VINAY VILAS PALACE WAS CONSIDERABLY EXPANDED IN THE 19TH CENTURY BY MAHARAJA VINAY SINGH.

A BIRD'S EYE
VIEW OF THE
PALACE
COMPLEX,
WHICH WAS
BUILT
IN THE
EIGHTEENTH
CENTURY.

THE 18TH CENTURY GOPAL BHAWAN AT
DEEG OVERLOOKS GOPAL SAGAR.
FACING PAGE: BHADON BHAWAN WITH ITS
GRACEFUL BANGLA ROOF.

WATER PALACE

Deeg

BUILT 18th century
LOCATION Deeg, Rajasthan
BUILT BY Raja Badan Singh
& successors
STYLE Mughal
DYNASTY Jat Dynasty

Once the capital of the rulers of Bharatpur, Deeg lies 36 kilometres to the north of Bharatpur town. Badan Singh, the first of the Jat rulers of Bharatpur, began fortifying the town in 1730. His son, Suraj Mal and grandson, Jawahar Singh were both prolific builders. They built the Water Palace and used it as a romantic summer retreat.

Inspired by the magic of the monsoons, the Water Palace of Deeg is built on two rectangular reservoirs, Gopal Sagar and Roop Sagar, which are connected by a charbagh (four-square garden). The palace itself consists of graceful pavilions that either face the garden or the reservoirs. An ingenious cooling system drew water from the huge reservoir and created interesting special effects to simulate monsoon showers and rainbows.

The principal pavilion, reflected in the serene waters, is the flat-topped Gopal Bhawan, with numerous balconies and overhanging kiosks. Flanking it on either side are the identical Sawan Bhawan and Bhadon Bhawan, named after the monsoon months, both shaped like upturned boats. A unique water-system creates a semicircle of falling water around them.

Nand Bhawan and Keshav Bhawan, the two other pavilions, face a lovely Mughal garden. On the roof of Keshav Bhawan were placed heavy metal balls that produced 'thunder' when water rushed up the hollow pipes concealed in the pillars and arches of the pavilion! At the back, balconies look out to Roop Sagar.

The old palace or Purana Mahal built by Badan Singh is situated at one end of the charbagh. It has numerous apartments; especially striking is the white marble Suraj Bhawan facing a small Mughal garden of its own, with intricate relief ornamentation and coloured inlay patterns as decorations.

The Deeg Water Palace, with its grand mansions, beautiful interiors and structures reflected in the water reservoirs, now stands sadly neglected.

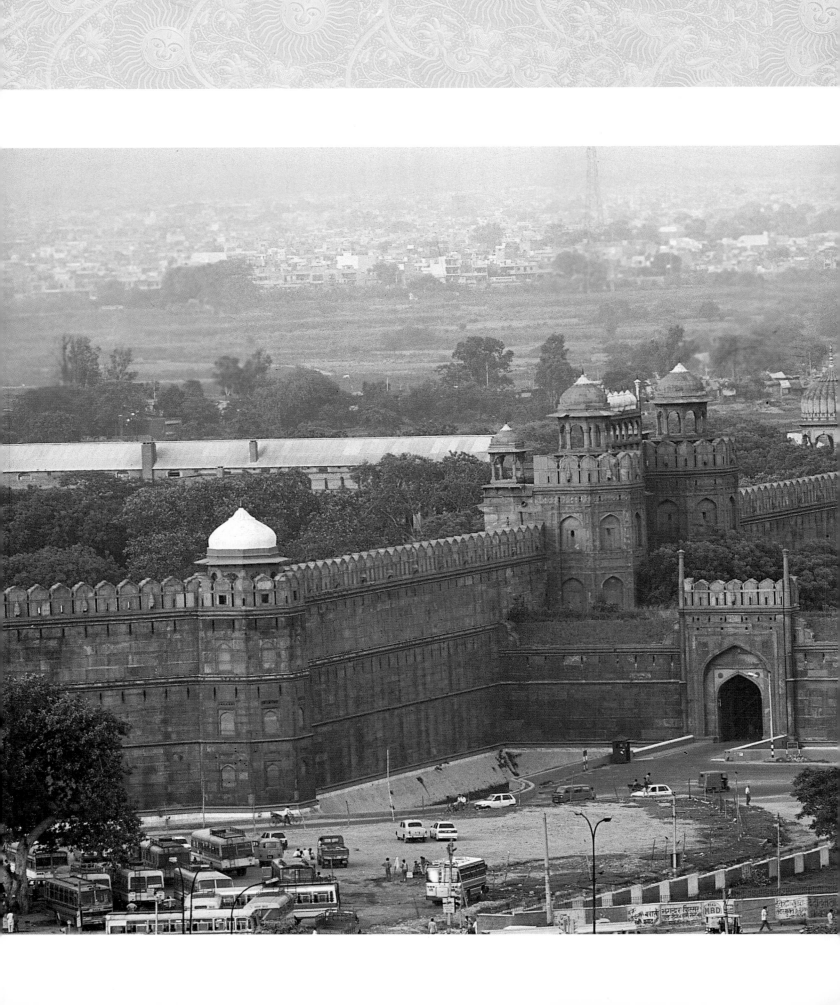

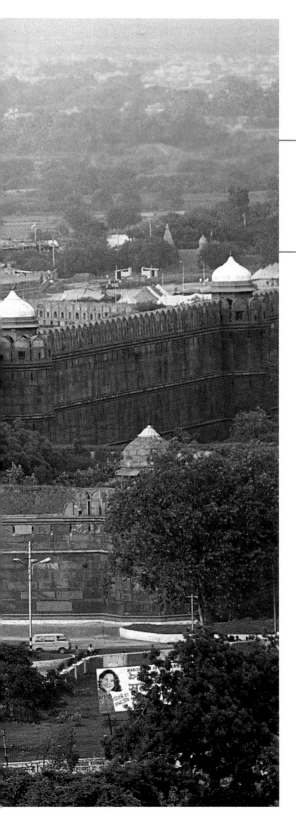

RED FORT
Delhi

BUILT 1639-1648
LOCATION Delhi
BUILT BY Emperor Shah Jahan
STYLE Mughal
DYNASTY Mughal

The majestic Lal Quila or the Red Fort is situated in Shahjahanabad, the city built by the Mughal emperor Shah Jahan when he shifted the imperial capital from Agra to Delhi. Work on the Lal Quila, which is situated on the western bank of the river Yamuna, began in 1639 and was mostly completed by 1648. It was Shah Jahan's principal residence and, after him, used by all the Mughal emperors. The Red Fort was raided twice: first by Persians invaders and then by the British who demolished many beautiful structures within the fort and replaced them with barracks.

The two main gateways to the fort are the Lahore Darwaza and the Dilli Darwaza. The main entrance is through the Lahore Darwaza on the west, which forms a part of massive sandstone fortification and is made up of dull pink sandstone. Just beyond lies the Chandini Chowk, the main street in Shahjahanabad. It used to have a tree-lined canal flowing down its centre and is a bustling market with a vibrant and chaotic bazaar today.

On the southern side of the fort is the Dilli Darwaza, which is connected to the Jama Masjid, India's largest mosque. The path from Lahori Darwaza leads to a vaulted shopping arcade known as Chhatta Chowk, originally a bazaar to service the palace. The arcade was also known as the Meena Bazaar, offering exclusive shopping for ladies of the court on Thursdays.

THE CENTRE OF IMPERIAL POWER FOR LONG, THE RAMPARTS OF THE RED FORT STILL DOMINATE THE SURROUNDING SKYLINE IN DELHI.

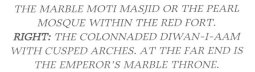

*THE MARBLE MOTI MASJID OR THE PEARL
MOSQUE WITHIN THE RED FORT.*
RIGHT: *THE COLONNADED DIWAN-I-AAM
WITH CUSPED ARCHES. AT THE FAR END IS
THE EMPEROR'S MARBLE THRONE.*

The Chatta Chowk terminates in an open square and at one corner is situated the Naqqar Khana or the drum house, a delicately carved red sandstone building. The drum house has four floors and it also served as a gatehouse, or Hathi Pol. All visitors, except the royals, had to dismount at this point.

The path from here leads to the Diwan-i-Aam or the hall of public audiences, a sixty-pillared hall made of red sandstone. The royal throne was placed here under a marble bangla-roof canopy and a base beautifully decorated with carvings and inlay work of semi-precious stones. The emperor sat here daily on a marble throne to hear complaints or disputes from his subjects and to deal with administrative matters. Behind the throne a pietra dura panels depicts the emperor calming animals, a symbolic representation of Shah Jahan's power over both man and the animal kingdom. A low bench in front of the throne was where his prime minister would sit.

Behind the Diwan-i-Aam, along the east wall of the fort, are a large formal garden and a row of five small palaces. Between the palaces and the garden was a stream, Nahr-i-Bihisht or stream of paradise, with a network of lotus shaped marble fountains. The palace on the extreme south is the Mumtaz Mahal, now a museum.

Close to the Mumtaz Mahal is the Rang Mahal or the palace of colours, once elaborately painted, where the emperor's chief queen resided .

The Nahr-i-Bihisht ran through the palace and ended in a lotus shaped central pool in the marble floor originally with an ivory fountain in the centre. The palaces are all built in the Baradari style.

On the northern side of the Rang Mahal is the Khas Mahal, which contains the imperial chambers. These include a suite of bedrooms, prayer rooms, a veranda and the Mussaman Burj, a tower from which the emperor would show himself to the people in a daily ceremony.

Built completely in white marble, the Diwan-i-Khas or the hall of private audiences is truly spectacular. The legendary jewel-encrusted Peacock Throne or the Takht-i-Taos adorned this hall before it was carried away by Nadir Shah to Iran in 1739. The complex also has the hammams or Royal Baths and to their west is Moti Masjid or the Pearl Mosque, which was built later as a private mosque for Emperor Aurangzeb.

Today the Red Fort is a symbol of India's sovereignty. Every year, on India's Independence Day, the Prime Minister addresses the nation and hoists the national tricolour from its ramparts.

MUHAMMAD BIN TUGHLAQ, THE WISE FOOL

A very learned man, Sultan Muhammad bin Tughlaq (r. 1325 - 1351) is often called a 'wise fool' because of his radical schemes that ended up as quixotic faliures. The best known is the transfer of the Delhi Sultanate's capital. In order to have better control over the newly conqured provinces in the South, he moved the capital from Delhi to Deogiri in the Deccan, renaming the city Daulatabad. But instead of just moving his offices he decreed that the entire population of Delhi be forcibly moved to Daulatabad. The plan failed because the arrangements for this herculean task were inadequate and, after two years, the capital had to be shifted back to Delhi. Many perished and it was said that Delhi was a ghost town for many years after the move back.

TUGHLAQABAD FORT

New Delhi

BUILT 14th century
LOCATION New Delhi
BUILT BY Sultan Ghiyasuddin Tughlaq
STYLE Indo-Islamic
DYNASTY Tughlaq

'*Ya base Gujjar, ya rahe ujar.*' (Let it either belong to the herdsmen or let it remain in desolation.) With these words, Sheikh Nizamuddin Auliya, the famous sufi saint, doomed Ghiyasuddin Tughlaq's capital, and to a visitor to these desolate ruins today, the curse certainly seems to have worked. It is said that the sufi mystic strongly disapproved of Ghiyasuddin's lack of religiosity and laid a curse upon Tughlaqabad which holds good till day.

Built in the early 1320s by Sultan Ghiyasuddin Tughlaq, the Tughlaqabad Fort is one of the earliest surviving forts in Delhi. The six square kilometer area occupied by this massive fort along a low ridge overlooks a wasteland. Its walls are made of gigantic, roughly cut, grey sandstone blocks fitted together with admirable precision. The massive ramparts, battlements and mammoth stonework of this fort indicate a high level of engineering skill.

There are a number of monuments within the precincts of this fort. On the southern side of the fort is a causeway that takes one across the now dry bed of a lake to the sandstone and off-white marble tomb of Ghiyasuddin Tughlaq. The tomb was built by Ghiyasuddin himself and is enclosed in a private courtyard with fortified walls. Its simple and elegant structure conforms to the Indo-Islamic style, which is the hallmark of the buildings belonging to the Sultanate period.

The Tughlaqs, who followed the Khiljis as the rulers of the Delhi Sultanate, were great builders and the city of Tughlaqabad and the Tughlaqabad Fort were their first major architectural achievement. The fort served as a defensive structure as well as the imperial capital of Ghiyasuddin Tughlaq, the founder of the Tughlaq dynasty.

GHIYASUDDIN TUGHLAQ'S TOMB. **FACING PAGE:** *THE CURSE FULFILLED: THE DESOLATE RUINS OF THE TUGHLAQ CAPITAL.*

THE FRONT FACADE OF THE JAGATJIT PALACE AT KAPURTHALA. THE
PALACE WAS MODELLED ON THE PALACE AT VERSAILLES IN FRANCE
AND WAS GRANDLY CALLED ELYSEE PALACE BY THE MAHARAJA,
JAGATJIT SINGH.

FRONT ELEVATION

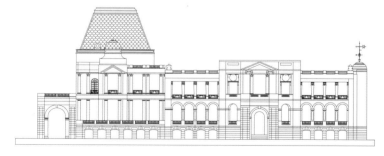

SIDE ELEVATION

JAGATJIT PALACE

Kapurthala

BUILT 1908
LOCATION Kapurthala, Punjab
BUILT BY Maharaja Jagatjit Singh
STYLE French Renaissance
DYNASTY Ahluwalia

In the northwest region of Punjab, amidst rich agricultural fields, is a corner that will be forever France. The capital of the former Sikh state of Kapurthala was the chief residence of the Ahluwalia family after the consolidation and conquest of the region by Jassa Singh in the second half of the 17th century. Sardar Jassa Singh, a contemporary of Nadir Shah and Ahmed Shah Abdali, annexed and consolidated a vast amount of territory. During the uprising against the British in 1857, his son Randhir Singh (r. 1853-70) remained unerringly loyal to the British and was permitted to retain his kingdom.

Kapurthala owes its extraordinary heritage to his great grandson, the eccentric Maharaja Jagatjit Singh (r. 1890-1947), an ardent Francophile. On his accession to the throne he invited three French architects to submit designs for his palace and awarded the commission to M. Marcel. Completed in 1908, the spectacular Jagatjit Palace or the Elysee Palace was modelled on Versailles with elements of Fontainebleu and the Louvre added on.

Like the Versailles, it is set in a grandiose park embellished with stone statuary and fountains. It is surrounded by villas meant for officials, which were modelled on those that were in vogue in the suburbs of Paris in the late 19th-century.

The pink-stucco exterior of the palace contrasts with the white detailing and high pavilion roofs. A grand staircase leads to a double-height Darbar Hall, now used as a library, with apartments on either side. The Darbar Hall has elaborate wooden brackets, jharokhas and railings with intricate wood carvings, and highly decorative wall surfaces with floral-motif panels.

In the eastern part of the palace is the dining room, decorated in 17th-century French style with blue lapis lazuli twin-columns with ornamental capitals, fire places, and gilded walls and ceilings. Priceless original Goblin tapestries hang from the walls. The apartment in the western side is a Louis XVI-style drawing room, complete with fine French furniture, objets d'art, and Renaissance-style painted scenes on the walls and ceiling.

The palace has now been converted into a school but sections of it are open to the public.

MOTI BAGH PALACE

Patiala

BUILT 19th century
LOCATION Patiala, Punjab
STYLE Indo-Saracenic
DYNASTY Sidhu Jat

Ruled by a string of flamboyant rulers in the 19th century, Patiala's name is a byword for everything larger than life. Thus the Patiala peg is a whopping measure of whisky, and it takes three times the usual amount of cloth to stitch the Patiala Salwar—salwar being the traditional attire of Punjabi women. Similarly, the huge Moti Bagh Palace made an English tourist gasp that it, 'makes Versailles look like a cottage'.

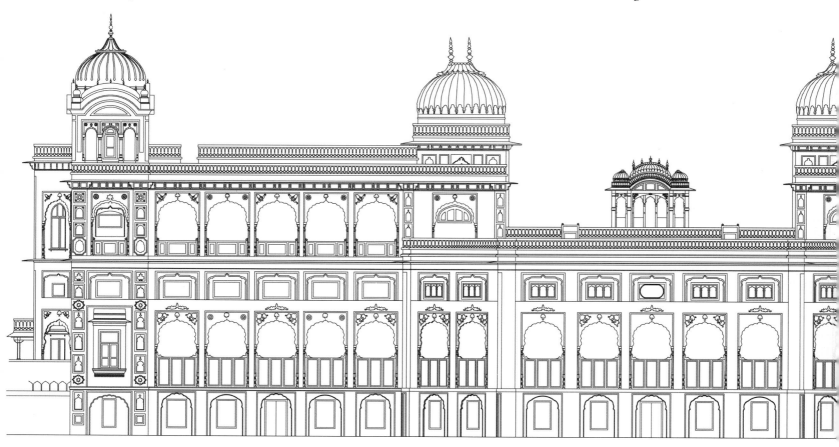

The Moti Bagh Palace, built in the late 19th-century Indo-Saracenic style, is in keeping with the flamboyant lifestyle of the maharajas of Patiala. Counted as one of the largest residences in Asia, the palace, with its fifteen dining halls, huge reception halls and innumerable rooms, sits amidst Mughal-style terraced gardens and water channels. The entire collection of chandeliers in the palace is said to have been bought at one go by Maharaja Mahendra Singh at a shop he casually entered while strolling in Calcutta. Not recognizing the maharaja, the shop owner is said to have cursorily dismissed him, and the annoyed maharaja bought everything in the shop and had it all transported in bullock carts to Patiala!

The terraces lead up to the Sheesh Mahal which was built by Maharaja Narendra Singh in 1847. The Sheesh Mahal houses a large collection of miniature paintings,

SHEESH MAHAL.

especially those from the famous Kangra school. Narendra Singh was a great patron of literature, music and the fine arts, and attracted many poets, scholars and historians to his court. Mughal and Rajasthani miniature paintings, as well as valuable manuscripts, also form a part of the museum collection. Notable is the *Gulistan Bostan* by Shiekh Sadi of Shiraz, which was acquired by the Mughal emperor Shah Jahan for his personal library and the payment for it was later made by his son Aurangzeb. Every page of the book is fully illustrated, with the drawings of flora and fauna etched in gold.

The medal gallery set up in the Sheesh Mahal has a large collection of medals and decorations, and is perhaps unmatched in the world for its richness and variety. On display are 3,200 Orders, Medals and Decorations, all collected by Maharaja Bhupendra Singh (r. 1900-1938). The earliest medals on display here are the 'Order of St Benedict of Aviz' and the 'Order of Christ' instituted by Portugal in the 12th century.

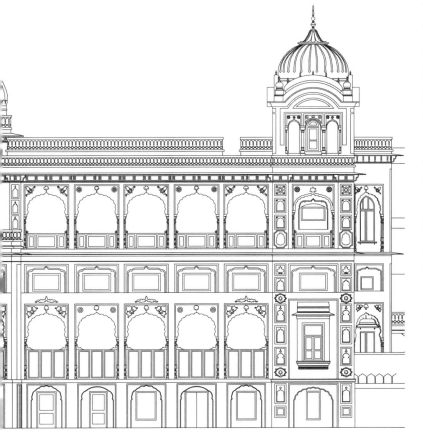

LEFT: *FRONT ELEVATION OF THE SHEESH MAHAL.*

QILA MUBARAK

Patiala

BUILT 1763
LOCATION Patiala, Punjab
BUILT BY Baba Ala Singh
STYLE Mughal & Rajput
DYNASTY Sidhu Jat

Patiala is situated between the rivers Sutlej and Ghaggar in Punjab, a prosperous state in north India which is known as the country's breadbasket. Patiala was an important princely state during pre-Independence India and Patiala city is among the newer cities of Punjab. It was founded by Baba Ala Singh around 1763 as a military stronghold on a site protected by rivers, hills and thick forests.

The present city has grown around the Qila Mubarak or 'the auspicious fort' built in 1763. The Qila Mubarak complex stands within 10-acre grounds in the heart of the city and contains the main palace which is also called the Qila Mubarak, the Ran Baas or the guest house and the Darbar Hall. The entrance to the palace is through an imposing gate, and its architecture is a synthesis of late-Mughal and Rajasthani styles. The complex has ten courtyards laid out along the north-south axis, and each courtyard is unique in size and character. Some are broad and stately, others have a formal garden and yet others are mere slits in the fabric of the building. The oldest part of the complex, the Qila Androon or the 'inner fort' was in a derelict state and is slowly being restored. Though the Androon is a single, interconnected building, it is referred to as a series of palaces, each carrying a name: Sheesh Mahal, Toshakhana, Jalau Khana, Chand Mahal, Rang Mahal, the treasury and prison. In a tiny portion of the complex is a small British style construction with gothic arches, marble fireplaces and built-in toilets perched on the painted Rajasthani roof!

The Rang Mahal and Sheesh Mahal are the painted and the mirror-work chambers respectively. The frescoes in Sheesh Mahal are amongst the finest in India. Painted in the second half of the 19th century, they consist of works of artists from the Rajasthani, Pahari and the Avadhi traditions. The mirror and gilt work in the Sheesh Mahal resembles the traditional Kundan jewellery in which 'diamonds', 'emeralds' and 'rubies' of coloured glass are set in gold-edged plaster work.

The Durbar Hall has been converted into a museum, displaying rare arms and armour, including the sword and dagger of Guru Gobind Singh, the tenth guru of the Sikhs, and the sword of the Persian invader Nadir Shah. The hall is built on a high plinth and was serviced by a network of tunnels. The façade gives the impression of a double-storey building with an 'upper storey' window and a balcony at the first-floor level, but the delicately worked wood and glass doors actually open into a huge 15-metre-high chamber. At the far end of the hall is a raised platform where the maharaja sat in state.

The Sard Khana was meant to provide relief from the summer heat. A deep well within acted as a wind tunnel, bringing cool air to the ground floor rooms and the basement.

The Lassi Khana or the kitchen is said to have served nearly 35,000 people everyday at one time, though, later, due to economic constraints this number was brought down to a 'modest' 5,000.

FACING PAGE: CHANDELIERS, WEAPONS AND PORTRAITS FORM A PART OF THE MUSEUM COLLECTION IN QILA MUBARAK.

BUILT BY THE NAMGAYAL RULERS, THE STOK PALACE REPRESENTS
THE FINAL PHASE IN THE EVOLUTION OF FORTIFIED PALACE
RESIDENCES CHARACTERISTIC OF THE LADAKH REGION.

ROYAL STOK PALACE

Stok

BUILT 1822-1836
LOCATION Stok (Ladakh), Jammu and Kashmir
BUILT BY King Tsepal Dondrub Namgayal
DYNASTY Namgayal dynasty

Ladakh is one of the three main regions comprising the state of Jammu and Kashmir, India's northern-most state, which borders Pakistan and the Tibetan plateau. Sometimes called the world's highest desert, it accounts for two-thirds of the state's area, its harsh terrain made beautiful by the emerald-green fields around its villages, clear blue skies and the ancient Buddhist monasteries silhouetted against the dramatic backdrop of stark cliffs.

Leh, Ladakh's principal town, was a commercial hub of a vibrant caravan trade route between Punjab and Central Asia, and between Kashmir and Tibet. Situated just 17 kilometre away from Leh is Stok, where the Royal Stok Palace has served as the residence of the rulers of Ladakh since 1834. Commissioned by King Tsepal Dondrub Namgayal in 1822, it was originally used as a summer palace after its takeover by the Dogra general, Zorawar Singh.

Built entirely by Ladakhi craftsmen, the main building was constructed in phases. Though smaller in scale than the palaces built earlier at Shey and Leh, the palace complex at Stok is architecturally one of the most important structures constructed in the Ladakh region. Built by the rulers belonging to the Namgayal dynasty, it represents the final phase of the evolution of fortified palace residences characteristic of this region.

The ingenious system of spatial planning has access passages leading to important rooms, including the royal apartments and the prayer chamber, which is arranged around multi-level interlinked courtyards. The otherwise austere five-storeyed main building has large decorative projected balconies at the upper levels.

The main palace has seventy-seven rooms spread over four storeys. The royal family occupies about twelve rooms; most of the historically significant sections have been converted into a museum where antiquities from the Himalayan region are displayed in an appropriate setting. The palace library contains a complete set of the Kangyur, the 109-volume compendium of the Buddha's teachings, which is printed on vellum rather than usual paper. The palace museum also has some rare Buddhist iconography, including priceless 14th-15th century tankas or painted scrolls, ornaments, royal costumes and headgear.

AGRA FORT

Agra

BUILT 1565-1573
LOCATION Agra, Uttar Pradesh
BUILT BY Emperor Akbar
& successors
STYLE Mughal
DYNASTY Mughal

Home to the famous Taj Mahal, Agra served as the capital of the Mughals during most of Akbar's reign, and that of Jahangir and Shah Jahan, before the latter shifted it to Delhi.

Work on the fort in Agra was started by Akbar in 1556 and construction continued till the time of his grandson, Shah Jahan. Agra Fort, also known as Lal Quila or Red Fort, is a massive red sandstone fortification, forming a crescent along the Yamuna riverfront. It contains within it a large number of buildings, ranging from the palaces built during Akbar's reign to 19th century barracks built by the British. A deep moat ran between the huge double ramparts, forming a circuit of more than two kilometers, watered by the Yamuna which originally came up to the fort's walls along the east side.

The fort is approached through the Delhi Darwaza on the west; a ramp leads to Hathi Pol (Elephant Gate) which is flanked by ornamented, semi-octagonal towers. To the south is the Akbari Darwaza, also known as Amar Singh Gate, decorated by brightly coloured tile-work on its towers. Inside is the only major surviving palace that dates back to Akbar's reign, the Jahangiri Mahal. Its red sandstone façade does not have a single window at the ground level, indicating that this was a zenana. In front is a pool carved out of single block of marble, with a Persian inscription dated 1611. According to local legend, the pool was filled and thousands

FLANKED BY TWO PAVILIONS, THE DIWAN-I-KHAS IS SITUATED BETWEEN A FORMAL GARDEN AND THE RIVER YAMUNA.

of red rose petals were sprinkled for empress Nur Jahan to bathe in. The palace has an ornate dome at the entrance, and the court is surrounded with apartments on three sides and a double-storeyed columned hall to the south. Screened balconies provide views of the river.

A small gateway from the Jahangiri Mahal leads to Anguri Bagh or the Grape Garden, with its square pool, raised walkway and geometric flower beds. There are underground chambers beneath, which could have been used either as a refuge from hot weather or as dungeons. The garden is surrounded by two-storey apartments of white marble at the centre of which is Khas Mahal or private pavilion which was built in 1636. An elegant marble hall with painted ceilings, it is reflective of Shah Jahan's style of architecture, and flanking it are two pavilions with

bangaldar roofs and small copper-covered domes. All the structures face the river.

Steps from the northeastern corner of Anguri Bagh lead to Musamman Burj, a double-storyed octagonal tower with a copper-sheeted dome, which has very

ABOVE: THE TAJ MAHAL AS SEEN FROM THE AGRA FORT.
BELOW: THE JAHANGIRI MAHAL: THE ONLY PALACE STRUCTURE THAT HAS SURVIVED FROM AKBAR'S TIME.

impressive views of the Taj Mahal. This exquisitely ornamented tower has a projected verandah and a rectangular chamber in white marble with breathtaking stone inlay panels and delicate jalis. This is where Shah Jahan, imprisoned by his son Aurangzeb, spent his last years, gazing at the Taj Mahal.

Next to the Musamman Burj is the Diwan-i-Khas, built by Shah Jahan in 1637. A lavishly appointed hall with delicate pietra dura work on its columns and brackets, and cusped arches fully covered in relief carving and inlay, it has two thrones: one black and one white. The black throne has a Persian inscription, dated 1603, carved on it. The Diwan-i-Khas too has a view of river, and this is where the emperor would conduct his court and watch elephant fights.

The impressive Diwan-i-Aam also dates from Shah Jahan's time and is open on three sides. Made from white marble, it has many columns with broad arches. A richly decorated alcove set in the eastern corner was where the fabled Peacock Throne was placed. There are two mosques in the complex: the Nagina Masjid (Jewel Mosque) built by Shah Jahan for the royal women, and the Moti Masjid or the Pearl Mosque which was his private mosque.

A VIEW OF THE PALACES, HALLS, GARDENS AND MOSQUES INSIDE THE FORT—SEAT OF MUGHAL POWER FOR NEARLY 150 YEARS.

FATEHPUR SIKRI

Fatehpur Sikri

BUILT 1571-1585
LOCATION Agra, Uttar Pradesh
BUILT BY Emperor Akbar
STYLE Blend of Mughal and Hindu
DYNASTY Mughal

Fatehpur Sikri or the city of victory is the finest example of the blending of Mughal and Hindu architecture, reflecting the secular vision of its builder, the Mughal emperor Akbar. Situated 37 kilometres from Agra, the city was built between 1571 and 1585 in honour of Shiekh Salim Chisti, the famous Sufi saint of the Chisti order, who had assured Akbar that he will be blessed with a son. It remained the Mughal capital for fourteen years, but then had to be abandoned because of water scarcity.

The city is laid out as a vast fortified rectangle, which encloses the sandstone ridge of a hill more than 2 kilometres long. Access to the city is provided by a straight road, lined with residences of nobles and serais or inns for visitors and travellers. The principal buildings are

AERIAL VIEW OF FATEHPUR SIKRI, BUILT BY AKBAR IN 1571 AS A TRIBUTE TO THE SUFI SAINT SALIM CHISTI.

THE DIWAN-I-KHAS OR HALL OF PRIVATE AUDIENCE. THE BUILDING MAY HAVE
SERVED AS THE AKBAR'S MEDITATION CHAMBER.

built mostly with locally quarried red sandstone, which was preferred by Akbar. The city and the imperial enclosure are a beautiful synthesis of Hindu, Jain and Islamic architecture, with features like carved jallis, brackets, domes and arches predominating.

The principle entrance is from the Agra Darwaza, which leads to the remains of Chahar Suq or the market square, and then beyond to the Naubat Khana, where the emperor's arrival was announced by the beating of drums.

Leading off the Naubat Khana is the imperial palace complex. In their originality of design, technical precision and the detail of decoration, the royal buildings in the complex are unparalleled in the history of Indian palace design. The first court is the Diwan-i-Aam, with a raised pavilion reserved for Akbar. A small doorway provided direct access to the Mardana, where Akbar's private and administrative business was conducted. At one end stands the Diwan-i-Khas, which, in spite of the name, probably did not function as an audience hall. It is surrounded by a balcony with low jalis and chajjas. In the middle of this room is a unique structure—a highly decorated tall pillar with a circular dais at the top, supported by carved brackets. This structure is supposed to have been used by Akbar to meditate as well as to listen to religious discourses.

Other buildings in the royal enclosure include the treasury or Daulat Khana and the Pachissi—basically, a giant game-board. It consists of a paved area marked out as two lines of squares, in the middle of which is a stone seat where people were used instead of pieces to play the game. To its west is the Panch Mahal, an elegant five-storyed pavilion where the royal ladies sat to watch the game. A small, exquisitely-carved pavilion stands in one corner; this was the interestingly named Turkish Sultana's House, probably the residence of one of Akbar's wives. Akbar's own sleeping chamber is an elevated pavilion with sloping roofs, called Khwabgah or the House of Dreams.

The zenana is connected to the Mardana by small doorways. The most impressive structure here is Jodha Bai's palace, the residence of Akbar's Rajput wife.

Beyond the zenana lies Birbal's house which was built in 1572. The walls of the house are covered with intricately carved patterns. The stables and the Ibadat Khana or the House of Worship are also part of the complex. A Jesuit church is another unusual feature of the palace complex, proof of Akbar's secular vision. The impressive Hiran Minar or Golden Tower stands 70 feet high with an octagonal chattri at the top.

ANUP TALAO (POND) GAVE THE PANCHMAHAL COMPLEX AN AIRY AND LIGHT FEELING EMPHASIZED IN THE DELICATE QUALITY OF CONSTRUCTION.

RAJ BHAWAN

Kolkata

BUILT 1798
LOCATION Kolkata, West Bengal
BUILT BY Governor Gen. Marquess
Wellesley, East India Company
STYLE Georgian

Not many cities in the world can boast of having a birth date—Kolkata has one. On August 24 1690, Job Charnock dropped anchor at Sutanuti on a rainy afternoon, and decided to set up the British trading headquarters in Bengal at that spot. The British bought the zamindari rights for three villages of Sutanuti, Kalikata and Govindpuri—the entire area comprising the future city of Calcutta from the Mughal emperor Aurangzeb for the paltry sum of Rs 16, 000.

In 1798, Calcutta welcomed Marquess Wellesley as its new Governor General. His lordship was determined to build a palace fit for the Governor General of India. Wellesley's palace—now the Raj Bhawan or the Governor's mansion—was built to the design of Captain Charles Wyatt of the Bengal Engineer. The completed palace became the butt of many a satire, but magnificent it was and still is, with a grand portico and a circular colonnade with a dome. Four wings, one at each corner of the body of the building, are connected by circular passages that air the entire building. These wings contained the private apartments, the council room and dining rooms. The palace has two halls. The lower hall, paved with dark, grey marble and supported by Doric columns, used to be the state dining room. It was called the Marble Hall and along its walls were arranged busts of twelve Ceasars, now no longer there. The hall above was the ballroom. Supported by Ionic columns, it has chandeliers suspended over dark, polished teakwood floor. The Throne Room houses Tipu Sultan's throne, which was captured and brought from Srirangapatnam in 1799.

The staterooms of the Government House, as it was then called, were lighted up for the first time for a grand ball to celebrate the Peace of Amiens. A sit-down dinner was arranged for 800 people and a brilliant firework display was organized on that day. Now, as the Raj Bhawan, the official residence of the Governor of West Bengal, it continues with its legacy in many respects. Many artefacts from Wellesly's time, including chandeliers, furniture and carpets are still on display.

FACING PAGE: THE NEO CLASSICAL ARCHITECTURE OF THE RAJ BHAWAN FEATURES MANY COLONNADED PORTICOES.

KANGLA & CAPITAL OF MANIPUR

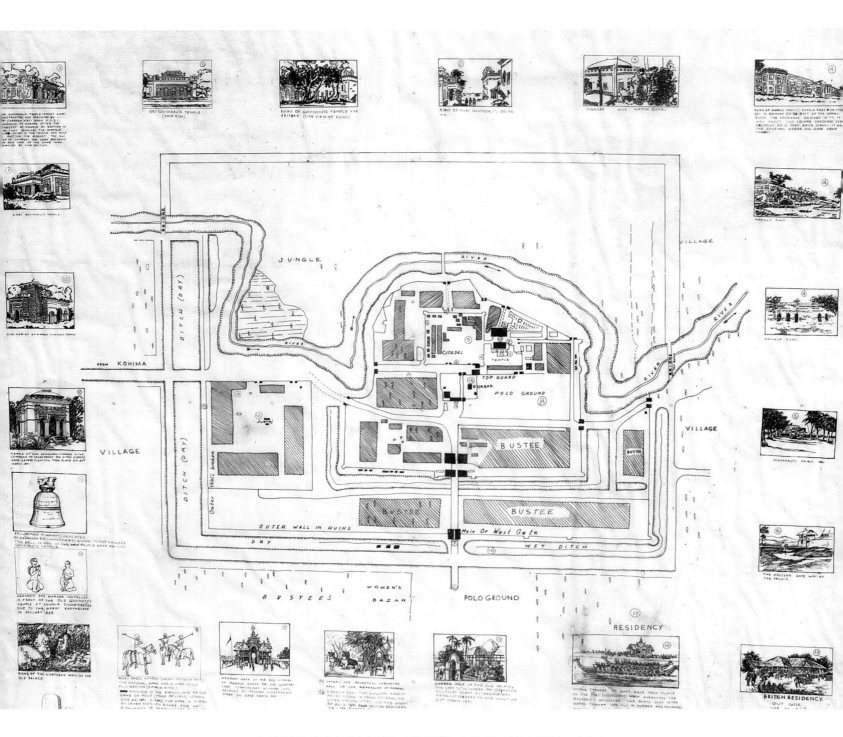

LAYOUT OF KANGLA AND ITS ENVIRONS BY THE IMPHAL RIVER.

KANGLA FORT

Imphal

BUILT Earliest reference in 1632
LOCATION Imphal, Manipur
DYNASTY Ningthouja dynasty

The Kangla Fort holds deep historical, cultural and religious significance for the people of Manipur. It was the capital of the kingdom of Manipur, and became the centre for administration, trade and commerce, as well as culture and religion, in the region. It is from the capital city of Kangla that the Ningthouja clan gradually expanded its power base to become the most dominant clan in Manipur.

Cheithrol Kumbaba, the royal chronicle of Manipur, makes many references to Kangla, describing how it was developed by successive monarchs. According to it, in 1632, King Khagemba (1597 - 1652), the conqueror of the Chinese, built a brick wall at the western gate of the Kangla Fort. The art of brick making was, in all likelihood, learnt from the Chinese who had invaded Manipur.

The initial tasks undertaken by the Manipuri kings in the Kangla Fort primarily related to the development and security of the fort.

Of particular archaeological significance are the ruins of 'Uttra' or the coronation hall inside the Kangla fort.

The building housing the coronation hall was destroyed in the Japanese air raids in the Second World War, and only the flight of steps leading to it and parts of the foundation remain. The polo grounds, situated in the southern part of the fort, are also of historical importance. Known as Manung Kanjeibung Manipuri, they were developed during the reign of King Marjit (r. 1813-19). According to Manipuris, the British introduced the game to other parts of India after they first picked it up here.

After the Anglo-Manipur war of 1891, the princely state came under British rule. The British military occupied the fort until the merger of Manipur with the Republic of India in 1948. The period of British occupation has contributed a significant layer to the architectural fabric of the fort, with military barracks and residencies. The residence of General Slim is of particular historical importance.

The Indian army occupied the fort till recently. It has finally been handed over to the state of Manipur and ambitious restoration plans are now on the anvil.

FALAKNUMA
Hyderabad

BUILT 1872
LOCATION Hyderabad, Andhra Pradesh
BUILT BY Nawab Vikar-ul-Ulmara
STYLE Indo-Saracenic
DYNASTY Asaf Jahi

The princely state of Hyderabad was the largest in pre-Independence India. This imperial city was the seat of the famous Nizams and evidence of its vanished elegance is to be found in its palaces, mosques, tombs and other monuments, as also in the dress, food and language of the Hyderabadis.

Nawab Vikar-ul-Ulmara, prime minister of Hyderabad, built the Falaknuma or Mirror of the Sky in 1872 and it was bought by the sixth nizam in 1897. It stands on top of the Kohi-Tur hill and has a Palladian façade with two open colonnades, one Ionic and one Corinthian. Built in the European style, the palace can be described as a blend of Italian and Tudor architecture.

The entrance hall has a white Italian-marble fountain and carved benches. A majestic staircase at the rear, with a carved balustrade that supports marble figures with candelabra, leads to the formal reception rooms with French tapestries and Victorian bric-a-brac.

The Darbar Hall is decorated in the French baroque style with heavily draped mirrors, chandeliers and a geometric parquet floor. The Falaknuma has huge Venetian chandeliers, reputed to be the largest in the world. It is said that it took six months to clean the 138-arm Osler chandelier, and the palace has forty of them! The dining hall could seat a hundred guests on a single table.

The library has a walnut carved roof, a replica of the one at Windsor Castle. In all, the palace has 220 lavishly decorated rooms and 22 spacious halls.

A STATE DRAWING ROOM AT FALAKNUMA.

GOLCONDA FORT
Hyderabad

BUILT 1518-1580
LOCATION Hyderabad, Andhra Pradesh
BUILT BY Sultan Quli Qutb Shah and
Sultan Ibrahim Qutb Shah
STYLE Bahamani
DYNASTY Qutb Shahi

The Golconda Fort is situated ten kilometers away from Hyderabad. Originally known as 'Mankal'—the name was derived from the word manik, meaning jewel—it is built on a plateau and served as the main fort of the Qutb Shahis, governors of the Bahmani kings. The Qutb Shahis asserted their independence in 1518 and Golconda became their capital. The Qutb Shahis ruled the Deccan for almost 171 years; they were known both for their patronage of learning and as great builders. Indo-Persian and Indo-Islamic literature and culture flourished during their rule, and Golconda became one of the leading markets in the world for diamonds, pearls, steel for arms and printed fabric.

Sultan Quli Qutb Shah started the task of replacing the 12th-century mud fort with a stone structure in 1518 and, sixty-two years and three rulers later, it was ready in 1580.

The architecture of the fort is a continuation of the Bahmani style, which itself had evolved from Tughlaq architecture. The fort is defended by three formidable fortification walls: the first, made of enormous blocks of granite, encircles the entire township; the middle wall surrounds the base of the hill; and the innermost encircles the highest ridge. The thickness of the outer walls ranges from 17 to 34 feet and it is punctuated by eighty-seven semicircular bastions, each 50 to 60 foot high.

DEFENDED BY THREE RINGS OF MASSIVE WALLS, THE RUINS OF GOLCONDA INDICATE WHAT WAS A BUSY, BUSTLING TOWNSHIP AND COMMERCIAL CENTRE.

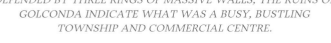

The huge 13-foot-wide and 25-foot-high, iron-spike studded Fateh Darwaza or the Gate of Victory, serves as the main entrance. A remarkable signaling device had been incorporated in the construction of the fort to transmit sound to all the guard-points within, whereby if any guard spied suspicious activity he could alert all other guards by a single soft clap that would lead to closing of all eight entry points to the fort.

The main road passes through the old treasury, now an archeological museum, and the once famous diamond cutting and polishing bazaar. The Habshi Gate, named after the Sultan's Abyssinian guards, had two massive arches with rooms at the top, and beyond it is the Naubat Khana (Drum House). To the north is the Jami Masjid, the magnificent Friday mosque built by the founder of the dynasty, Sultan Quli Qutb Shah, in 1518 and just after that is the Bala Hisar Gate. This ceremonial entry gate to the royal complex has various Hindu motifs and is reached after climbing 360 steps. The mythical figures carved on it indicate Hindu influence. Similar carving can be found in other parts of the fort walls. The Bala Hisar marks the inner area of the fort; the complex contained the royal palaces, assembly halls and workshops.

Within a walled enclosure in the fort is the Boab Hathion ka Jhaad (Elephant Tree), said to have been brought by the sultan's Abyssinian guards 700 years ago. The fort also contains the ruins of the Qutb Shahi palaces, the most impressive being the Rani ka Mahal—a vaulted hall on a raised terrace decorated by beautiful floral arabesques. The fort still has traces of a water channel system, the water being brought to the top of the hill after being checked for poison at various levels.

Just below the summit is an elegant mosque built by Sultan Ibrahim Qutb Shah, and an ancient Hindu Mahakali temple built into a cave. At the top is the three-storeyed Durbar Hall (Throne Room) with a rooftop pavilion, with spectacular views of the entire fort and its surroundings. A wide, secret tunnel, now closed, could transfer the royalty fourteen kilometres beyond to safety.

DIAMONDS OF GOLCONDA

It was during the reign of the Qutb Shahi kings that Golconda became world famous as a trading, polishing and cutting centre for diamonds, though diamonds were never mined in Golconda proper. In 1645, Jean Baptiste Tavernier, a French jeweller, visited Golconda and chronicled the story of the diamond finds in the Kollur group of mines along the Krishna river, in the territory ruled by Golconda.

Koh-i-noor, the world's most famous diamond, was mined here in the year 1656, during the reign of Sultan Abdullah Qutb Shah. It was presented to the Mughal emperor Shah Jahan while still uncut, weighing 787 carats. In the intervening centuries it passed through many hands and now adorns the crown of the British monarch, weighing 106 carats. Other famous diamonds mined at Golconda include the 277-carat Nizam diamond, said to be only a piece of the 440-carat mother diamond. The Hope diamond—believed to be part of the legendary Blue diamond that had a 'curse' attached to it—also came from Golconda and was sold by Tavernier himself to the French king Louis XIV in 1642.

VIJAYNAGAR

Hampi

BUILT 1336
LOCATION Hampi, Karnataka
BUILT BY Harihara and Bukka Rai
STYLE Mix of different Hindu styles
DYNASTY Sangama, Saluva, Tuluva,
Aravidu

As the might and the influence of the Tughlaq dynasty (1320-1414), which ruled over the Delhi sultanate in north India, waned, many new independent states began to emerge.

In 1336, two brothers Harihara and Bukka Rai, founded the kingdom of Vijaynagar, which went from strength to strength to become a mighty empire that covered the greater part of south India. Founded in the early 14th-century on the banks of the Tungabhadra river, the capital of the rulers of the Sangama dynasty, Vijaynagara or the 'City of Victory', was built to showcase their imperial might.

The capital of three generations of rulers for more than 200 years, the city of Vijaynagara, or Hampi, as it is now called, flourished during the reign of Krishna Deva

HUGE GRANITE BOULDERS DOMINATE THE HAMPI LANDSCAPE.

Raya (r. 1510-1529) and Achyut Deva Raya (r. 1529-1542). It was abandoned after the defeat of the Vijaynagara forces in 1565 by the combined armies of the Deccan sultanates.

A UNESCO World Heritage site, Vijaynagara is situated to the south of a rocky gorge, its ruins spread over an area of about 25 square kilometers or 10 square miles. The site is divided into the royal centre and the sacred centre.

The urban core of the city or the royal centre was fortified, and housed the palace of the rayas (kings) and the residences of the elite members of the court. It was separated from the sacred centre by an irrigated valley through which old canals and waterways still run. Gateways mark the principle roads that led into the royal centre. Much of it is divided by thin high walls and tapering constructions of tightly fitted granite blocks. Standing inside these enclosures are the remains of residential and administrative structures, and bathing tanks, wells and water channels, indicating a sophisticated system of water collection and disposal.

The Ramchandra Temple, standing at the core of the

royal centre, was meant for the king's private worship, its walls beautifully depicting the epic story of the Ramayana through sculptures. The temple was the nodal point between different enclosures: on one side were the structures for the public and ceremonial life of the king, on the other lay the residential buildings.

To the southeast of the temple is the huge multi-storey granite Mahanavami platform, its sides covered with carvings of soldiers, elephants, scenes of royal receptions, dancing girls and musicians. The platform was used by the rayas to view the Mahanavami celebrations and pre-war ceremonies. To the west is a large floor area, all that remains of the hundred-columned assembly hall which has been described by Domingo Paes, the Portuguese envoy to Vijayanagar in the 16th century. The remains could also be of the hall

described by the 15th-century Persian envoy Abdul Razzaq, in which case this would be one of the earliest examples of an audience hall in a Hindu palace.

There are many structures clustered together, which evoke images of splendour and use sophisticated design techniques. There are two tanks which, in all likelihood, were meant for ritualistic purposes. The large-stepped tank, constructed with green chlorite, was fed by a water chute, which formed a part of the extensive hydraulic system that serviced the royal centre. The Lotus Mahal, which probably served as a council chamber for the king, is laid out on a symmetrical plan with projections on each side. A pleasing blend of

Hindu and Islamic architecture, this two-storeyed pavilion is decorated with plasterwork birds and flowers, and stone brackets shaped as mythical beasts or *yalils*. Immediately outside the Lotus Mahal enclosure are the Elephant Stables. This imposing structure has eleven square chambers that once housed the royal elephants. In the sacred centre lies the grandest of all religious monuments—the Vitthala Temple. Though it is not known who built the original temple, it was enlarged in the 16th century by Krishna Deva Raya and Achyuta Deva Raya. The Vitthala temple represents the high point of Vijaynagara art and architecture.

THE RUINS OF A BRIDGE OVER THE TUNGABHADRA RIVER.
FACING PAGE: *NAGA STONES, VIRUPAKSHA TEMPLE.*

FORT ST GEORGE

Chennai

BUILT 1640
LOCATION Chennai, Tamil Nadu
BUILT BY East India Company
STYLE Neo-classical

Chennai, formerly Madras, owes its genesis to two determined East India Company merchants, Francis Day and Andrew Gogan, who acquired a sandy tract of land said to belong to a farmer called Madrasan. The company negotiated the deal in 1639 with the local nayaks (governors) at Poonamalee. On this strip of land they established a 'factory' or a trading post that grew into the seat of British power in the East. Completed on St George's Day, 23 April 1640, this fortified settlement came to be known as Fort St George.

The area's history goes back a long way, as is evident from the 9th-century Parthasarathi temple at Triplicane, one of the first villages to be acquired by the East India Company and now a bustling suburb of Chennai.

The old, solid and staid enclosure of Fort St George was built with the simple aim of protecting the trading outpost and merchandise of the English. The first building or 'factory' was also called the fort-house. It took thirteen years to build and was enclosed with a brick and mud wall faced with laterite, a locally available stone.

In due course, the settlement grew, spilling outside these walls and this necessitated an outer wall. The outer fort, then, surrounded the new 'White Town', with its English, Portuguese and Armenian inhabitants. The northern gate of this new enclosure led to the marketplace, beyond which lay the old 'Black Town'- the Indian settlement of weavers, dyers and merchants.

The inner fort was square in plan, while the outer fort was oblong—walled in only on three sides and defended by the River Elambore on the fourth. By 1710, the fort was full of houses, neatly lined along the streets. The original fort-house was rebuilt further to the east as a neo-classical building, part of which still exists as the core of the Secretariat building.

The French occupied Fort St George in 1746 and had possession of it for three years. The English recovered it and immediately began strengthening it. The sloping ramparts and battlements for gun emplacements were designed and constructed in 1750. These ramparts form an irregular pentagon and are further reinforced by a ring of earthen walls that slope down into a moat. The original drawbridges that led to the five gates of the fort have been converted to roads.

BRITISH NEO CLASSICAL STYLE IS PREDOMINANT IN THE STRUCTURES INSIDE FORT ST GEORGE.

Within the fort is the neo-classical secretariat building, the seat of the Tamil Nadu state government, and, behind it, the Legislative Council Chambers. These elegant buildings built between 1694 and 1732, with their classical lines and facades of gleaming black pillars, are said to be among the oldest surviving British constructions in India. The 148-foot-tall flagstaff was erected by Governor Elihu Yale in 1687. Yale, who had begun his career as a clerk in East India Company, went on to found the Yale University in the United States.

To the south of the legislature building is the St Mary's Church. Built between 1678 and 1680, it is the oldest Anglican church in all of Asia. Both Arthur Wellesley, who later became the Duke of Wellington, and Robert Clive lived in Fort St. George and their residences are still standing.

Near the large parade ground to the north is the Fort Museum, which was built in the 1780s as the Public Exchange. It is a treasure house of war memorabilia, old lithographs of Madras and paintings.

GINGEE FORT

Gingee

BUILT 15th - 16th century
LOCATION Gingee, Tamil Nadu
DYNASTY Vijaynagar Nayakas

Situated in the state of Tamil Nadu in south India, Gingee Fort, also known as Senji Fort, is a superb example of the military engineering skills of the Nayakas. The Nayakas were the principal governors of the Vijaynagara kings in this region and in the 16th century proclaimed their autonomy. The fort complex comprises of three citadels perched on three rugged granite hills—Krishnagiri, Rajagiri and Chandrayandurg.

They form a triangular area, spreading out approximately a mile from north to south. Huge 60-foot-thick rampart walls and a ditch, almost 80 feet wide, go around the whole complex. With a perimeter of three miles, this enclosed area forms the lower fort. It has two main entrances, called the Arcot or Vellore gate and the Pondicherry gate.

Built by the Nayakas between the 15th and 16th century, the fort has had a varied history, occupied in turn by the Adil Shahi sultans, the Marathas, the Mughals, the French and the British. In spite of various invasions, the ruins, spread all over the three hills, are quite spectacular.

The most prominent among the ruins are the granaries, mosques, arcaded halls and tanks. Many temples, mostly dedicated to Lord Vishnu, also survive. Among these the Venkataramana Temple in

TEMPLES IN GINGEE FORT. FIRST BUILT BY THE NAYAKAS, GOVERNORS OF THE VIJAYANAGAR EMPIRE, THE FORT WAS IN TURN OCCUPIED BY ADIL SHAHI SULTANS, THE MARATHAS, THE MUGHALS, THE FRENCH AND THE BRITISH.

THE 700-YEAR-OLD FORT SPRAWLS ACROSS THREE HILLS.

the outer fort area is the largest. It was built by Muthialu Nayaka in the 17th century. Near the gateway are panels depicting scenes from the Ramayana and the *Vishnu Purana.*

The Nayaka royal complex is situated within the inner fort, which is entered through two gateways. The Durbar Hall is located on Krishnagiri hill, along with two small temples: the Ranganatha Temple and the Krishna temple. The most prominent structure in the complex is the Kalyana Mahal, which was built for the royal ladies with apartments on the four sides of a square tank. The stucco decorations on its walls outside are typical of the Vijayanagar period.

A six-storeyed pyramidal tower with arcades has a large hall on each floor. Visible within and around the complex are foundations of royal residences. A line of small chambers, possibly stables for horses, faces a parade ground between the royal residences and Kalyana Mahal.

Two impressive granaries form a part of the royal enclosure; also visible is a complex network of natural springs and tanks that provided water to the complex. One of the tanks is dedicated to Raja Thej Singh, a brave Rajput chief who was killed in a battle against the Nawab of Arcot.

NAYAKA PALACE
Thanjavur

BUILT 14th - 16th century
LOCATION Thanjavur, Tamil Nadu
STYLE Hindu
DYNASTY Nayakas, Marathas

The city of Thanjavur, or Tanjore as it is commonly known, lies in the Kaveri delta, often referred to as the 'rice bowl' of the south Indian state of Tamil Nadu. The capital of three powerful dynasties—the Cholas (9th-13th century), the Nayakas (1535-1676) and the Marathas (1676-1855)—for nearly a thousand years, this magnificent town was the political and cultural centre of the region. The town is dominated by the magnificent Chola monument, the Brihadishvara temple, which is situated in the Shivganga Fort that dates back to the Nayaka period.

Built by the Nayaka ruler, Sevappa Nayaka, in the mid-16th century, the quadrangular Shivganga Fort lies to the southwest of the old city. The monumental granite Brihadishvara Temple temple was completed in 1010 by Rajaraja Chola I and dedicated to Lord Shiva. Now a UNESCO World Heritage Site, the temple basement is covered with inscriptions

18TH CENTURY STUCCO FIGURES IN MARATHA DURBAR HALL.

that are an invaluable repository of information about life during the Chola rule and their systems of governance.

The royal palace, also known as the Nayaka Palace, stands in the middle of the city. Built by the Nayakas as their residence and subsequently added to by the Marathas, the complex consists of a large square court in the centre, surrounded by open pavilions and multi-storeyed structures. At one end is a pyramid-like structure that was probably a temple. Just outside the palace complex is a seven-storeyed observation tower, now minus its roof.

Built by Shahji II in 1684, the Maratha Durbar hall has elaborately painted pillars and ceilings. The designated area for the Maratha throne consists of a wide canopy, supported by wooden pillars and decorated with pieces of glass, standing on a green granite base. The Maratha palace is situated in the southern part of the complex, overlooked by the Durbar hall, its walls decorated with thick plaster ornamentation. The palace has been converted into a museum and exhibits the personal collection of Serofji II, a scholar and patron of arts. Close to it lies the Sangeet Mahal or music hall, with special acoustic features.

The Nayaka Durbar hall was restored in the 1950s and converted into a museum. Now called the Rajaraja museum, it has a collection of the famous Chola bronzes and stone idols dating from the 7th to the 19th century.

PATTABHISHEKAM: 18TH CENTURY MURALS AT THE ENTRANCE OF SARASWATI MAHAL LIBRARY.
***BELOW:** CEILING OF THE MARATHA DURBAR HALL.*

PADMANABHAPURAM PALACE

Padmanabhapuram

BUILT 18th century
LOCATION Padmanabhapuram,
Tamil Nadu
REBUILT BY Maharaja Martanda Varma
STYLE Traditional Kerela
DYNASTY Travancore

Padmanabhapuram palace is the finest example of Kerala's distinctive wooden architecture. From 1590 to 1790, Padmanabhapuram, city of the 'Lotus Born' (Padmanabha, an aspect of Vishnu) was the capital of the Travancore kings. The capital was then shifted to Trivandrum (Thiruvanathapuram) and Padmanabhapuram was used as a summer residence.

Set amid lush hills, green paddy fields and perennial rivers, the palace is laid out in a sequence of four adjoining walled compounds, which move from public to private zones. The palace was rebuilt during the reign of Martanda Varma (r. 1729-58) maharaja of the erstwhile Travancore state.

The main entrance to the palace complex is reached after crossing a large courtyard reserved for public ceremonies. The Padipura or main gate is a traditional structure with a decorated gabled roof. Facing it, in the second courtyard is the audience hall, which occupies the upper level of a two-storeyed structure. Supported by large circular wooden columns, it has a profusely carved wooden ceiling with ninety different inverted flower designs.

To the north stands the Navaratri Mandapam, the dance hall, which is supported by stone columns with complex carvings of female figures and other motifs. A small shrine dedicated to Saraswati, the goddess of knowledge, stands to the south of the hall.

The private zone begins with the third court and the Uppirika Malika, the tallest structure in the complex, stands here. It is a four-storey structure with the chambers placed one above the other. The third court also contains the Thai Kotlaram or the queen mother's residence. Built in 1550, this is the oldest building in the complex. It has intricately carved wooden pillars fashioned from jackfruit trees. Earlier, the floor used to be polished with hibiscus flowers to achieve a red gloss.

Other structures in this court are the Lakshmi Vilaram and Pilamuttu Kottaram for the women of the court; the Uttupura, the two long dining halls, one above the other; and the Homapura—a building with a stepped tank meant for ritual use.

FACING PAGE: A SECTION OF THE FIRST BUILDING IN THE ROYAL COMPOUND IN PADMANABHAPURAM PALACE, WHICH HOUSES A RECEPTION HALL AND AN AUDIENCE HALL.

THIRUMAL NAYAKA PALACE

Madurai

BUILT 1636
LOCATION Madurai, Tamil Nadu
BUILT BY Thirumalai Nayaka
STYLE Indo-Saracenic
DYNASTY Nayaka and Marathas

The ancient city of Madurai lies on the banks of the river Vaigai in Tamil Nadu. Sangams, the legendary gatherings of poets and writers held over 2,000 years ago, which have given Tamil literature some of its most celebrated works, were held here.

Megasthenes, the Greek diplomat and envoy to India in the 3rd century BC, gave a glowing account of Madurai in his famous work *Indica*. Home to the famous Meenakshi Temple, the city was the capital of the Pandya rulers from the 7th to the 13th century. The city flourished under Pandya rule when it was a major trading hub with contacts with Greece, Rome and the Middle East. It later became the capital of the Vijaynagar empire under the Nayakas in the 16th and 17th centuries.

After establishing themselves at Tanjore, the Marathas absorbed Madurai into their own kingdom sometime in the late 17th century. The Thirumalai Nayaka palace, built by Thirumalai Nayaka in 1636, is an evocative reminder of the wealth and power that the Nayakas commanded in the region. The original palace complex was four times the size of the existing structure. What remains is the main palace where the king used to live.

This palace consisted mainly of two parts, namely Swargavilasa and Rangavilasa. In these two parts, there is the royal residence, theatre, shrine, apartments, armoury, palanquin place, royal bandstand,

TOP: FINE STUCCO WORK OVER THE ARCHES IN THE DANCE HALL.
LEFT: THE COURTYARD WITH ORNATE PLASTERWORK COVERING THE ARCADE.

quarters, pond and garden. King Thirumalai Nayak celebrated many festivals, like the Sceptre festival, Navarathri, Chithirai festival, Masi festival and the float festival.

Large parts of the palace complex collapsed in the 19th century and it was partially restored by Lord Napier, the governor of Madras between 1866 and 1872. The Durbar Hall is reached through a large colonnaded courtyard called the Swarga Vilasam or the Heavenly Pavilion. Solid circular piers support broad arches, with alternating pyramidal and vaulted roofs. To its west lies the throne chamber with a large raised octagonal dome over it; thick plaster ornamentation covers the arches and vaults with motifs of birds, animals and flowers, and squat columns on both sides create an interior vista.

The Nritya Sabha or the dance hall has a large arcaded space with a raised platform on the eastern side, and a double-height ceiling. It is heavily ornamented with plasterwork of animals and birds.

FACING PAGE: THE BEJEWELLED AMBA VILAS PALACE ILLUMINATED BY 50,000 LIGHT BULBS.
BELOW: *THE ORNATE NATAKSHALA (THEATRE) IN THIRUMAL NAYAKA PALACE.*

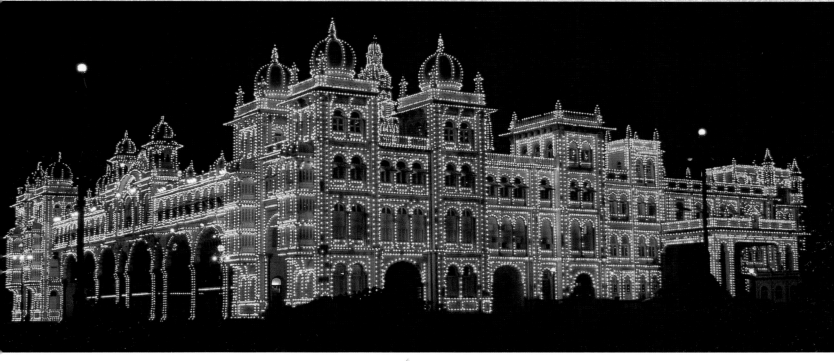

AMBA VILAS PALACE

Mysore

BUILT 1912
LOCATION Mysore, Karnataka
BUILT BY Maharani Vaninilasa Sannidha
STYLE Indo-Saracenic
DYNASTY Wodeyar

Situated among fertile fields which are encircled by wooded hills, Mysore was the capital of the Wodeyars, the governors of southern Karnataka under the Vijayanagar kings. The Wodeyar dynasty ruled almost uninterrupted from 1399 until Independence, except for the 38-year rule of Haider Ali and his son Tipu Sultan in the 18th century. After the British reinstalled them in 1799, the Wodeyars undertook to transform Mysore into a model city, and build a fortified residence for themselves. Most of the palace complex was destroyed during a fire in 1897 and Vaninilasa Sannidha, the Queen-Regent at the time, commissioned designs for the new Amba Vilas Palace. This beautiful palace, built in a lively Indo-Saracenic style by the architect Henry Irwin was completed in 1912, during the reign of

Krishnaraja IV (r. 1902-46). It was later extended in 1932.

The Mysore Palace was the first in India to make use of cast-iron construction columns and roof-frames, which were manufactured in Glasgow and then shipped to India. The imposing Jaya Martanda gate on the eastern side of the palace compound serves as the main entrance. The façade of the palace is dominated by a huge portico of polished grey granite columns which support cusped arches. A twelve-sided tower, capped by a gilded dome with a miniature chattri on top, dominates the background, along with other domed

AMBA VILAS IS A MÉLANGE OF HINDU, ISLAMIC, MOORISH AND INDO-SARACENIC ARCHITECTURAL STYLES.
LEFT: *THE CURRENT WODEYAR MAHARAJA OF MYSORE PERFORMING POOJA ON VIJAYA-DASHMI DAY.*

towers which are grouped below it. The entire façade looks spectacular when illuminated with more than 50,000 light bulbs on festivals and weekends.

Inside, a richly decorated staircase ascends between marble walls of different colours and the teak ceiling has carvings of many Hindu deities. At the upper level is the Durbar Hall, gilded in gold and turquoise. More than 50 meters long, it is divided into aisles by squat, tapering columns decorated with gilded leaves and lotus petals. Painted images of eight goddesses, including Chamundeswari, adorn the rear walls, as also do portraits of different kings painted by the famous artist, Raja Ravi Varma. The golden throne is now brought out only during Dussehra celebrations. The Durbar Hall leads into the private audience hall, the Amba Vilasa. This breathtakingly opulent hall has a stained-glass roof imported from Glasgow, its central section supported by cast-iron columns and arches. The floor panels are inlaid with semiprecious stones in the Mughal style and the magnificent setting is completed by glittering chandeliers and silver doors.

In the middle of the palace complex is a courtyard with carved stone columns and, to its west is a part of the original zenana of the old palace, which has now been converted into a museum displaying the royal art collection. To the south is the Kalyana Mandapa or the Marriage Pavilion, another cast-iron structure with a stained-glass octagonal dome embellished by peacock motifs.

GWALIOR FORT

Gwalior

LOCATION Gwalior, Madhya Pradesh
STYLE Rajput
DYNASTY Tomar/Scindia

In the autumn of 1528, Babur went to Gwalior and, despite opium sickness, visited the palaces of Man Singh and Vikramaditaya. According to his diary, he found the buildings wondrous. A 16th-century Persian chronicler described the fort as, 'the pearl in the necklace of castles of Hind'.

The Gwalior Fort stands on a sheer, 300-foot-high sandstone hill in central India and is said to have been inhabited since the 6th century. From the 8th century on, it served as the seat of power of a succession of Rajput rulers—whose shrines still exist at the top of the hill—until it was captured by Sultan Iltutmish in 1232. In 1398, Bir Singh Deo captured Gwalior and established the Tomar dynasty.

The most powerful of the Tomar kings was Raja Man Singh (r. 1486-1516); his palace, Man Mandir, is decorated by beautiful blue and yellow tile-work, incorporating animal figures of peacocks, parrots, ducks and crocodiles holding lotus buds. It has one of the most glorious exteriors of all the Rajput palaces. The Tomars lost control of the fort in 1518, and the Maratha Scindias gained control of it in the 18th century. The fort stayed with them till the merger of the Gwalior State with the Indian Union, after Independence.

The fort is best approached from the Urvashi Gate, where twenty-one figures representing the Jain tirthankaras (apostles), are carved into the rock

THE GREAT EASTERN FACADE OF THE MAN MANDIR PALACE IN THE FORT HAS HIGH, FLAT, UN-PIERCED AND HIGHLY DECORATED WALLS, PUNCTUATED BY MASSIVE ROUND TOWERS WHICH ACT AS REINFORCING BUTTRESSES.

ABOVE: DETAIL FROM MAN MANDIR PALACE.
RIGHT: OLD JAIN SCULPTURES INSIDE THE FORT.

face. Man Mandir Palace, situated at the extreme edge of the fortress, forms a part of a group of four palaces built by Man Singh during his reign. Man Mandir, also known as Chit Mandir or painted palace, is so designed as to have a forbidding and daunting affect on the approaching visitor. The great eastern façade of the palace rises a hundred feet above, and the ascent to the palace passes through six gates.

The palace walls are flat and un-pierced, punctuated by massive round towers. Relief is provided by cupolas which, according to Babur's account, were originally gilded with copper.

The royal residence in Man Mandir is divided into two courtyards, with the façades elaborately carved and decorated with tiles. A secret passage to the north connects it to Vikramaditya's palace which, though bigger, is not so elaborate. Among the apartments in the palace is the exceptional baradari—a large hall covered with a dome and supported by eight carved columns. The third palace, Gujari Mahal, was built by Man Singh for his tribal wife, Mrigananya, around 1510. Built on the mardana pattern, it is rectangular in plan with a large central court. Jharokas and double-height chattris are placed on the four corners, while most of the interior apartments, which have largely collapsed, lead to a small courtyard.

164 165

JAI VILAS PALACE
Gwalior

BUILT late 19th century
LOCATION Gwalior, Madhya Pradesh
BUILT BY Jiyaji Rao Scindia
STYLE Italianate
DYNASTY Scindia

The Prince of Wales visited India in 1876, and the Scindias of Gwalior celebrated his visit by building one of the most impressive royal residences, the Jai Vilas Palace.

Designed by Colonel Michael Filose, this vast Indo-Saracenic palace is laid out around a big square court. The approach is through intricately worked cast-iron gates of the four wings, three wings are for offices and apartments, and the fourth, which is marked by raised rooftop turrets signaling its importance, contains the state apartments.

This wing has the magnificent Darbar Hall, which is approached by a double staircase with delicate crystal balusters. Decorated in the grand 18th century classical style, it has golden curtains and crystal furniture; two huge crystal chandeliers, said to weigh 4,000 kg each, hang from its ceiling. The strength of the ceiling is said to have been tested by building a mile-long ramp up to the roof and walking twelve elephants on it.

The much talked about solid silver tabletop train, used to deliver after-dinner drinks and cigars to the royal guests, is displayed in the Banquet Hall on the lower floor. A part of Jai Vilas is now run as a museum while the rest remains the residence of the royal family.

FACING PAGE: THE GIGANTIC CRYSTAL CHANDELIERS IN THE DURBAR HALL.

AN ELEGANT DRAWING ROOM IN JAI VILAS

A CANNON IN THE PALACE LAWNS

MAHESHWAR FORT
Maheshwar

BUILT 18th century
LOCATION Maheshwar, Madhya Pradesh
BUILT BY Ahilya Bai Holkar
STYLE Maratha Wada
DYNASTY Holkar Dynasty

Picturesque Maheshwar stands on the bank of Narmada, one of India's seven holy rivers.

An important Hindu pilgrimage centre, Maheshwar's history goes back at least 4,000 years. It lies on the site of the ancient city of Mahishmati.

The Mughal emperor Akbar first built the ramparts of the Maheshwar Fort in 1601. Later, when the Mughal empire was in decline, Malhar Rao Holkar, the founder of the house of Holkars, was rewarded with the gift of territories comprising the Indore region by the Peshwas of Pune. His daughter-in-law, the revered Maratha queen, Ahilya Bai Holkar, succeeded him. Sir John Malcolm, in his *Memoirs of Central India*, described her as a, 'female without vanity... exercising in the more active and able manner, despotic power with sweet humanity...' She made Maheshwar the capital of her kingdom in the late-18th century, and built the fort, which stands on an isolated hill on the northern bank of the Narmada River, dominating the landscape of the town.

A beautiful fan-shaped stairway leads from the riverfront to the royal complex inside the fort. It is entered through an intricately carved courtyard, wherein stands a statue of Ahilya Bai, described by

MAHESHWAR, WHICH LIES ON THE SITE OF THE ANCIENT CITY OF MAHISHMATI, HAS A HISTORY GOING BACK TO EARLY ANTIQUITY. THE RAMPARTS OF THE FORT WERE FIRST BUILT BY THE MUGHAL EMPEROR AKBAR.

Malcom as, 'one of the purest and most exemplary rulers that ever lived.' The palace inside the complex has now been converted into a museum displaying heirlooms of the Holkar dynasty. A special exhibit is a small shrine on a palanquin that is carried down from the fort during the annual Dussehra celebrations.

The memorial cenotaph in the complex is dedicated to Ahilya Bai's son, with a sculpted panel depicting the chilling story of his death. Ahilya Bai is said to have ordered his death after receiving complaints of his atrocities from her subjects. She had him trampled by a pair of elephants.

The fort has many temples dedicated to various incarnations of Lord Shiva, including the impressive Ahilyeashwar Temple built in 1798. Also within the fort is the REHWA Society, a co-operative of local weavers promoted by the Holkar family, which is famous for weaving gossamer fine Maheshwari cotton and silk textiles.

SUNSET ON THE BANKS OF THE NARMADA.

MANDU

Mandu

BUILT 6th century-10th century
LOCATION Mandu, Madhya Pradesh
STYLE Indo-Islamic
DYNASTY Paramara, Khilji,
Malwa dynasty

Perched on a crest at the edge of the Malwa plateau, and surrounded by deep woods, the deserted fort of Mandu is spread over an area of 23 square kilometres and is situated in one of India's most picturesque sites.

According to evidence from ancient texts, and from an inscription discovered at Talanpur, near Khushi, the hill fort of Mandu was raised in 6th century AD. Dating back to 535 AD, the inscription refers to the fort as Mandapadurga. By the end of the 10th century, the fort was under the control of the Paramara rulers. It was captured by Alauddin Khilji from the last Paramara ruler, Mahalak Deo, in 1305 and after that it became the capital of the central Indian province of Malwa.

In 1401, the fort was captured by a governor of the Delhi sultanate, Dilawar Khan, who started an independent line of Malwa sultans. His son, Alap Khan, shifted his capital from Dhar to Mandu, and Mandu came to be known as Shadiabad, the city of joy. Mandu remained the capital of the Malwa rulers till 1531, when it was captured by Bhahadur Shah of Gujarat; it then fell to the Mughals in 1560. In 1696 the Marathas captured the fort and it was abandoned later. Some restoration work was done on it on the orders of the British viceroy Lord Curzon who visited the fort in 1902.

The sultans of Malwa built beautiful palaces, pleasure pavilions, mosques and lakes here, and they can be grouped into two clusters—the Royal Enclosure and the Village Group. The Delhi Darwaza serves as the principal entrance to the royal monuments, which are clustered together. Other buildings are spread all over the plateau, many with names that link them to the Paramara times.

A PAVILION ON THE ROOF OF THE JAHAZ MAHAL.

Towering over the royal enclave are two palaces: the Jahaz Mahal and the Hindola Mahal. The Hindola Mahal or the swinging palace has massive inward sloping walls which give the impression that the building is swaying. Built in the 15th century, it consists of a main hall with a projecting entrance; its plain façade is embellished by tracery work on the arched windows. Facing it is the Champa Baoli, a step-well complex with a labyrinth of subterranean rooms, serviced by an ingenious ventilation system which kept them cool for the ladies of the harem.

To the east are Gada Shah's house and shop, said to belong to an ambitious Rajput chieftain of the Mandu court. The 'shop' is actually an audience hall, and the house, a well-planned double-story structure with water channels and fountains, still bears faint traces of paintings of Gada Shah and his wife. Dilawar Khan's mosque is said to be the oldest extant structure in Mandu. It was built in 1405 using stones and pillars of Hindu and Jain temples that stood there earlier.

Jahaz Mahal was built between 1469 and 1500 by Ghiyas-ud-din, the fifth sultan of Malwa. Situated between two manmade lakes, Munja Talao and Kapur Talao, this pleasure palace looks like an anchored ship, especially during the monsoons. It is said to have been inhabited by the 15,000 women of his harem! The pleasure-loving sultan also had a contingent of 500 beautiful young Turkish and Abbysinian female bodyguards. The palace has three large halls arranged in a line; a long flight of stairs—the ship's 'anchor'—leads to the rooftop, offering fabulous views from the pavilions there. The ones on the ends have pyramidal vaults and small domes, while the one in the centre has a bigger dome, adorned by blue and yellow tiles and a small pool in front that is fed by a water channel. A beautiful bathing pool at the northern end of the palace is colonnaded on three sides.

Many important monuments lie between the royal enclosure and Sagar Talao, Mandu's largest lake. The most famous is the palace of Baz Bahadur (r. 1555-62), the last sultan of Malwa who was defeated by the Mughals in 1561. The inscription over the main entrance assigns the construction to Sultan Nasiruddin (r. 1500-11). The main portion of the palace has rooms and vaults that face an open courtyard with a square pool in the centre. Just to the south is Roopmati's pavilion, named after the beautiful singer who Baz Bahadur fell in love with and married. Situated at the crest of the hill, the pavilion is approached by steep steps and offers spectacular views of the countryside.

Some of the fort's best-preserved buildings can be found around the village. Built in 1440, the tomb of Hoshang Shah, Malwa's most powerful sultan, was the first marble mausoleum to be built in India. An inscription on the door records the visit of Shah Jahan's architects in 1659 who were obviously inspired by its perfectly proportioned structure when they designed the Taj Mahal.

The spectacular Jami Masjid, said to be inspired by the great mosque of Damascus, has three large domes and fifty-eight smaller ones. Work on it started during the reign of Hoshang Shah and took three generations to complete. The Ashrafi Mahal madarsa was a theological seminary built by Sultan Mahmud in 1443.

After Mandu fell to the Mughals, it was used primarily as a halting place en route to Deccan. The only palace built by the Mughals was the Neelkanth Mahal. It was built in 1574 at the site of an old Shiva temple. Emperor Jahangir spent seven months here in 1616.

ORCHHA

Orchha

BUILT 16th century
LOCATION Orchha, Madhya Pradesh
BUILT BY Raja Bir Singh Deo
STYLE Bundela
DYNASTY Bundela Rajput

On a rocky island looped by the river Betwa, lies the medieval city of Orchha, the capital of the Bundela Rajputs from 1501 to 1738. The golden period of Orchha began with the reign of Bir Singh Deo in 1605, who befriended the young prince Salim, Akbar's son and the future Mughal emperor Jahangir. Bir Singh Deo was rewarded with the gaddi or the throne of this region. He ruled till Jahangir's death in 1627. During this period he is credited with building magnificent palaces and temples in Orchha and in the small town of Datia.

One of the distinguishing features of the palaces of Orchha is that they are not all extensions of a single garh-palace (fort-palace), but are three separate garh-palaces built next to each other. They are built on a similar pattern, in a distinct style known as Bundela architecture.

The three palaces in Orchha (and one in nearby Datia) differ from the majority of Rajput garh-palaces in being symmetrical in their planning. This is attributed by some scholars to the influence of Indo-Islamic architecture, though these palaces seem to be more influenced by the principles of ancient Hindu architecture. Their layout is based on the Mandala pattern as prescribed in the *Manasara*, which was composed between AD 500 and 700. Rudra Pratap, the founder of the dynasty, started building the first palace, which is now the Ram Raja temple, around 1520. This is a four-storeyed square structure, with a central open courtyard. This plan is repeated in the second palace, the Raj Mandir. However, the architects experimented a bit and put in a number of small chattris (cupolas) at the topmost level.

This design element was abandoned and not used by Bir Singh Deo when he built the largest palace in Orchha, Jahangir Mahal, named after his patron the Mughal emperor. In order to relieve the monotony of the high outer walls, it seems that the architects decided to raise the towers but only till the second storey and then place chattris on top. This sandstone palace with 132 chambers, and an equal number of subterranean side rooms, is profusely decorated with ornate jallis and blue tile-work on the outer façade.

FACING PAGE: THE CHATURBHUJA TEMPLE CAN BE SEEN IN THE DISTANCE, AND A SECTION OF THE RAJA MAHAL IN THE FOREGROUND. FOLLOWING PAGES 178-179: THE CHATTRIS (CENOTAPHS) OF THE ORCHHA RULERS ON THE BANKS OF BETWA RIVER.

GOVIND PALACE

Datia

BUILT 16th century
LOCATION Datia, Madhya Pradesh
BUILT BY Raja Bir Singh Deo
STYLE Bundela
DYNASTY Bundela Rajput

Fifteen miles northwest of Orchha is the Govind Palace at Datia, an example of Bundela architecture at its most sophisticated. Datia, a town of great antiquity, finds mention in the epic Mahabharata as the town Daityavakra.

The seven-storeyed palace was built entirely of stone and brick by Bir Singh Deo in 1614. The overall design here is the same as the Orchha palaces, with multi-level construction around a central chowk. However there is a difference: at the centre of the chowk is a square, five-storeyed tower, containing the royal chambers. This central structure is connected with bridges to the lower storeys of the ranges, and rises above the upper storeys. Within the palace are some fine wall paintings of the Bundela school.

One of the ways in which the Bundelkhand palaces differ from other Rajput palaces is that the zenana is not distinct from the mardana, but a part of the main palace. This has lead some scholars to propound that entire palaces were only zenanas, meant for the royal women. Which leads to the obvious question that if these palaces were zenanas, then where were the mardanas?

The more rational explanation seems to be that during the early periods of the Rajput school of architecture, the garh-palace was probably meant only for a select few—the women of the royal family and some more members of the immediate family. It was later, when the more distant male relatives of the king, and the nobles, ministers, courtiers and guards, began to be admitted into the palaces, that the need for a distinct, separate zenana was felt. These started being built as the garh-palaces became more public.

FACING PAGE: THE PINNACLE OF BUNDELA ARCHITECTURE, GOVIND PALACE IS UNIQUE IN THAT IT HAS A MULTI-STOREYED TOWER STANDING IN THE MIDDLE OF AN OPEN COURTYARD.

LAXMI VILAS PALACE
Vadodara

BUILT 1878
LOCATION Vadodara (Baroda), Gujarat
BUILT BY Sayaji Rao III
STYLE Indo-Saracenic
DYNASTY Gaekwad

In the heart of the city of Baroda, now known as Vadodara, stands the exquisite Laxmi Vilas Palace set in 700 acres of land.

The palace is home to the Gaekwads, the ruling family of the erstwhile Baroda State. They rose to power in the wake of the Maratha expansion during the 18th century, and, in the century that followed, they cemented their power by treaties and statecraft, in the process securing their control over vast territories in the heart of Gujarat.

The Laxmi Vilas Palace is a delight to behold, with its neat 500-foot façade, its curved balconies and windows, its towers, turrets and upper pavilions with Bangla roof. Architecturally, it represents a confluence of Indian, Persian and European influences, and is built in the Indo-Saracenic style. Charles Mant was commissioned to design and build the palace as the royal residence in 1878 by Sayaji Rao III (r. 1875-1939), the most accomplished of all Gaekwads. It was completed twelve years later by Robert Fellowes Chisholm and is a testimony to the modern and progressive attitude of the rulers of Baroda.

The palace stands in a vast park dotted with huge marble sculptures, vases and massive bronze sculptures of animals; it can be accessed through huge arched gateways.

THE FLOOR OF THE INDO-ITALIAN STYLE ENTRANCE HALL OF LAXMI VILAS IS COMPOSED OF SEVERAL DIFFERENT KINDS OF MARBLES.

The general plan of the palace is very traditional, with three functional zones—the public reception rooms including the Darbar Hall, the apartments for the king and his attendants, and the zenana. Each of these zones consists of a quadrangle with a courtyard in the centre and its own entrance with a portico. The interiors of the palace are quite eclectic, as seen from the gilded mosaic on the walls of the vestibule, the marble sculptures by Felici, Venetian chandeliers, period furniture and stained glass. It has been aptly remarked that there is a small patch of the world in every part of the palace. The Darbar Hall, one of the largest in the world, for instance, has crystal chandeliers, stained glass windows depicting the marriage of Lord Ram and Sita, and a geometric wooden ceiling done in the Moorish style. Projecting jharokas rest on wooden brackets designed to resemble musicians. The huge entrance lobby to the maharaja's apartments has a beautiful Grecian urn in the centre and an inner court has a marble pool with a spectacular fountain and statues surrounding it.

A part of the palace is now the Maharaja Fatehsinh Museum. It was originally a schoolhouse for Maharaja Pratap Singh and a miniature train would bring the royal children daily from the palace to the school. The engine still stands on the museum porch as a reminder of those indulgent days. The museum has an impressive collection of paintings by the great 19th-century artist Raja Ravi Varma, who had a special studio built for him in the palace, and lived there for twelve years.

The Gaekwads made Baroda one of the most progressive states in India, complete with hospitals, a university, a college of music, banks, an agricultural corporation and mobile libraries. They were the leaders in initiating social reforms and promoting the arts in the city, making it a cultural power house.

THE NEO-ISLAMIC STYLE CEILING AND STAINED GLASS WINDOWS IN THE DURBAR HALL.

NEW PALACE

Morvi

BUILT 20th century
LOCATION Morvi, Gujarat
BUILT BY Lakhadizaj
STYLE Art Deco
DYNASTY Jadeja

Morvi is situated in the Saurashtra peninsula, the western-most part of Gujarat, and is now known mostly for its floor and roof tiles. This small principality prospered in the mid-19th century and its most influential ruler was the modern and progressive Waghji (r. 1879-1922).

His son Lakhadizaj (r. 1927-47) built the spectacular New Palace in the art deco style in 1931, in this remote corner of India. The palace is built on a square plan, with two interior courts that are enclosed with colonnades.

On the north side is the main entrance with marble columns and a tower shaped like a pyramid in the centre. The entrance leads into a large hall with marble walls and a recessed ceiling with a brilliant painting of the sun god on his chariot drawn by four horses, painted by the Polish artist Stefan Norblin. The concealed lighting makes the gold in the painting gleam, thereby heightening its effect.

The ground floor of the palace has a formal reception and entertainment areas, along with rooms for guests. The formal dining hall is set between the two courts and has a bar where the colour pink dominates. The bar has a long counter with a mural of nude women in repose at the back and pink leather barstools in the front.

On the southern side of the complex is the gymnasium, with a large swimming pool that is watered by a fountain set in a semicircular recess with dramatic lighting and paintings on either side.

The upper floor has the king's and queen's private apartments. The maharaja's bedroom has a built-in canopy with a bed, raised on a black marble podium and a fireplace with an ornate mantelpiece. The maharani has a big en-suite bathroom recessed into a marble-shell back wall—all in true art deco style. Another staircase leads to the reception area and the banquet hall, done in tones of blue, and to another private bar, which has a rose-pink marble fountain in the middle.

The palace continues to be the private residence of the royal family and is rarely opened to the public.

FACING PAGE: A BEDROOM IN THE NEW PALACE WITH A LARGE FRESCO BY THE POLISH ARTIST STEFAN NORBLIN.

GLOSSARY

bagh garden

bala hisar upper fortress

bangla roof or vault curved like the typical Bengali hut

baoli stone step-well

baradari ('twelve doored') typical Mughal-style twelve pillared pavilion

bazaar market street

bhawan hall, house or abode

brahmin the priestly caste, which is uppermost in the hierarchy

burj fortified tower

chahar suq open square with market on four sides

charbagh ('four-gardens') formal walled garden

chhajja angled eave

chhatri royal umbrella; roof-top ornamental pavilion with dome or vault; funerary monument

chhatta see chhatri

chowk square courtyard, main square in a city

darbar royal audience

darwaza door or entrance gate

daulat khana treasury

diwan-i-aam hall or court of public audience

diwan-i-khas hall of private audience

durg fort

ganesh pol elephant gate

garh fort

giri hill

hamam bathhouse

harem women's quarters in the king's household

hathi pol elephant gate

ibadat khana house of worship

jali, jalli ornamental pierced or latticed stone-screen

jami masjid mosque, especially for Friday prayers

jauhar voluntary immolation by women after their men went to the battlefield to fight till death

jharokha decorative projecting balcony with a dome or vault roof

kalyana mandap hall for marriage or other festive occasions

khas mahal private pavilion

khwabgah royal sleeping chamber

kot, kotla fort

kund tank or pond

madrasa Islamic theological college

mahal palace, pavilion, apartment

maharaja great king

mandir temple, abode

mardana men's quarters

masjid mosque

minar minaret, light tower

muharram Shiite month of mourning

musamman burj octagonal tower

naqqar khana drum house

naubat khana guard house

nawab governor, ruler

nayaka governor

nivas, niwas palace, abode

nizam ruler

pol gate

qila fort

raja, rana, rao, rawal ruler

rang mahal muliti-coloured pavilion

raya emperor

sabha assembly hall

sagar ocean, lake

sheesh mahal mirrored room or pavilion

stambha pillar

sufi a saint, broadly within the Islamic tradition

suq marketplace

suraj pol sun gate

takht seat, throne

talao pool, lake

tazia ornately decorated tower of wood, metal and paper carried by Shia muslims during
   Moharram

torana temple portal with decorated lintel

tripolia triple arched ceremonial gate

vilas, vilasa palace

zenana designated area of a palace or house where women live in seclusion

BIBLIOGRAPHY

Alikhan, Raza, *Hyderabad 400 Years (1591-1991)*, Zenith Services, Hyderabad, 1991.

Ghose, Aruna, Ed. *Eyewitness Travel Guides: INDIA*, Dorling Kindersley, New Delhi, 2002.

Issar, T.P., *Royal City: A Celebration of the Architectural Heritage & City Aesthetics of Mysore*, Bangalore, Marketing Consultants, 1991.

Keay, John, *India: A History*, Harper Collins Publisher India Pvt. Ltd., New Delhi, 2000.

Losty, J.P., Calcutta, *City of Palaces: A Survey of the City in the Days of the East India Company, 1690-1858*, INTACH, 1990.

Manchanda, Bindu, *Jaisalmer: City of Golden Sands and Strange Spirits*, Harper Collins Publishers India Pvt. Ltd., New Delhi, 2001.

Michell, George & Martinelli, Antonio, *The Royal Palaces of India*, Thames & Hudson Ltd., London, 1994.

Modi, Sumesh, *Impressions of a Forgotten City*, Heritage Trust, Baroda and ASI Publication, 2004.

Naravane, M.S., *Forts of Maharashtra*, APH Publishing Corporation, Delhi, 1995.

Punja, Shobita, *A Capital Story*, HECS, INTACH, New Delhi, 2003.

Singh, A.P., *Forts and Fortifications in India*, Agam Kala Prakashan, Delhi, 1987.

Singh, Dhananajaya, *The House of Marwar*, Roli Books, New Delhi, 1994.

Tillotson, G.H.R., *The Rajput Palaces*, Oxford University Press, New Delhi, 1999.

Todd, James, *Annals and Antiquities of Rajasthan*, MN Publishers, New Delhi, 1978.

FACING PAGE: RELIGIOUS TRADITIONS AND CEREMONIES HAVE ALWAYS BEEN AT THE CORE OF THE INSTITUTION OF ROYALTY.

ISBN: 978-81-7436-381-7

© This edition Roli & Janssen BV 2008
Third impression
Published in India by
Roli Books in arrangement with
Roli & Janssen BV, The Netherlands
M-75, Greater Kailash-II Market
New Delhi 110 048, India.
Ph.: ++91-11-29212271, 29212782
Fax: ++91-11-29217185
Email: roli@vsnl.com
Website: rolibooks.com

Editor: Himanshu Bhagat
Design: Inkspot
Layout: Naresh Mondal

Printed and bound in Singapore

DETAIL FROM SAMODE PALACE.

PHOTO CREDITS

Amit Pasricha: p. 18
Anne Garde: pp. 21, 28-29, 122, 134, 138-139, 166, 167 (top),
    168-169, 182-183, 184-185, 186
Corbis: pp. 10-11, 12-13, 47, 48-49, 72
Dheeraj Paul: pp. 56-57
Ganesh Saili: pp. 2-3, 32-33, 51, 76
Courtesy, Hotel Ahilya Fort: pp. 170-171
Jean-Louis Nou: pp. 17, 86-87, 118 (top), 121
Karoki Lewis: pp. 74, 100-101, 102-103
Nicholas Courier: p. 82
Pankaj Rakesh: p. 14
Pramod Kapoor: pp. 42-43
Private Collection: pp. 22-23, 36, 50, 188
Roli Collection: pp. 4-5, 7, 20, 24, 26-27, 37, 38-39, 40-41,
    44, 52-53, 54, 55, 58-59, 60 (top), 62-63, 64, 66-67, 68,
    70-71, 78 (bottom), 79, 80, 81, 84-85, 88-89, 90-91,
    92-93, 94-95, 96-97, 98-99, 104-105, 106-107, 110,
    112-113, 114, 114-115, 126-127, 128 (top), 128 (bottom),
    129, 130-131, 132, 133, 167 (bottom), 176, 192

Rajpal Singh: p. 78 (top)
Sanjay Singh Badnor: pp. 30-31
The Royal Archives, HM Queen Elizabeth II, Windsor
    Castle: pp. 34-35
The British Library, India Office Library,
    London: pp. 108-109
The Hindu Images: p. 136
Toby Sinclair Pg 61, 111, 116, 117, 124, 140-141, 143,
    144 (bottom), 144-145, 147, 162-163, 164 (top), 164-165,
    172-173, 175, 178-179, 180
V. Muthuraman Pg 148-149, 150, 151, 152 (bottom), 152-153,
    154, 156-157, 157, 158, 159, 160, 161

Lustre Press acknowledges INTACH for providing
line drawings of Sheesh Mahal, Patiala and
Jagatjit Palace, Kapurthala.